Brave Parenting

BRAVE PARENTING

A Buddhist-Inspired Guide to Raising Emotionally Resilient Children

By Krissy Pozatek, LICSW

WISDOM PUBLICATIONS • BOSTON

Wisdom Publications
199 Elm Street
Somerville, MA 02144 USA
www.wisdompubs.org

Library of Congress Cataloging-in-Publication Data
Pozatek, Kristine.
  Brave parenting : a Buddhist-inspired guide to raising emotionally resilient children / by
Krissy Pozatek.
    pages cm
  Includes bibliographical references and index.
  ISBN 978-1-61429-089-6 (pbk. : alk. paper) — ISBN 1-61429-089-X (pbk. : alk. paper) — ISBN
978-1-61429-109-1 (eBook)
  1. Child rearing. I. Title.
  HQ769.P8285 2014
  306.874—dc23

                          2013029845

18 17 16 15 14
5 4 3 2 1

Author photo by Kelly McCracken. Cover design by Phil Pascuzzo.
Interior design by Gopa&Ted2, Inc. Set in Dante 11/14.5.

Wisdom Publications' books are printed on acid-free paper and meet the guidelines for
permanence and durability of the Production Guidelines for Book Longevity of the Council
on Library Resources.

Printed in the United States of America.

 This book was produced with environmental mindfulness. We have
elected to print this title on 30% PCW recycled paper. As a result, we have
saved the following resources: 14 trees, 6 million BTUs of energy, 1,202
lbs. of greenhouse gases, 6,522 gallons of water, and 438 lbs. of solid waste. For more information, please visit our website, www.wisdompubs.org. This paper is also FSC® certified.
For more information, please visit www.fscus.org.

For my parents
For my daughters

To cover all the earth with sheets of leather—
Where could such amounts of skin be found?
But with the leather soles of just my shoes
It is as though I cover all the earth!

And thus the outer course of things
I myself cannot restrain.
But let me just retrain my mind,
And what is left to be restrained?

—SHANTIDEVA, *The Way of the Bodhisattva*

Table of Contents

Part IV: Two Trails Side by Side

A Letter to Parents

In this book, I will refer to life's journey as a trail, a rocky path symbolizing all of the challenges we face in everyday life—struggles with family, with friends, with school, or with pursuits outside the home, or simply the difficulties of managing our daily fluctuation of thoughts and emotions. Sometimes, however, when walking a trail, we encounter even bigger obstacles: a loss, a trauma, a diagnosis, or other setback. These jagged boulders and sharp rocks at first seem insurmountable but actually offer profound gratification when successfully navigated. In order to travel our paths gracefully, we need a way to work with the obstacles that we will all inevitably encounter, as well as the emotions that run through us like a river.

In *The Way of the Bodhisattva*, eighth-century Buddhist sage Shantideva tells us that we can either lay down leather wherever we step so we don't cut our feet, or we can make our own moccasins to protect us on our path. In this book, I adapt this metaphor to parenting in order to illustrate the widespread hovering and overinvolvement parents engage in today, as many parents are busy cushioning their children from any discomfort. Unfortunately, this leather laying makes our children more dependent and less resourceful and impedes their emotional maturation process. Instead, we can create a home environment that fosters moccasin building so our children have the internal resources and emotional resilience necessary to navigate their life-trail and get where they need to go.

After working for many years in adolescent wilderness-therapy programs, I have seen many struggling young people find gratitude, self-esteem, and mastery when successfully navigating their life obstacles. The solution is not removing or softening difficulties and discomforts from our children's lives, it is compassionately encouraging them to be brave—

teaching our children to work with their own rocks and boulders and seeing their bruises and scrapes as fodder for maturation. In every obstacle we face there is a corresponding lesson, insight, awareness, or opportunity for growth if we allow our struggles to teach us, rather than fight and resist them. This is the maturation and moccasin-building process.

In wilderness therapy, I have observed that kids find relief when they stop looking for an exit, an escape, or a rescue from a parent and instead face their problems and struggles head-on. They begin to feel capable and resourceful. Deep down we all want to solve our own problems, because that is how we grow wiser and more confident in life. Yet most of us won't if we know there is still some cushion, some way out, someone to blame, or someone to rescue us. Although adversity has merit, no one really pursues it voluntarily.

Living with the grit of Mother Nature provides indelible lessons. Because the only safety net (aside from the satellite phone) is the group's ingenuity, each individual is challenged to problem-solve, be resilient, and work together. Though not always comfortable, living within the natural world actually returns a light to young people's eyes and brightens their spirits. Individuals have to face nature head-on, submit to its terrain, and endure the weather patterns, whether pure sunshine or vicious storm. Ultimately kids learn that life is simple in the wilderness—they readily see that they are not in control and learn that they get out of the experience what they put in to it.

Parenting, however, is complicated. There are so many balls to juggle, so many philosophies and perspectives to consider, so many feelings to attend to, and so many doubts. The obstacles are multifaceted and the solutions less clear. It's overwhelming, and so parents tend to cope through action: taking over a task, fixing, solving, and overmanaging.

Yet I believe that parenting can be much easier than we think. We don't have to do it all. In fact, "not doing" allows our kids to face natural consequences that teach much more enduring and lasting lessons than us nagging or lecturing. For example, when a child forgets a rain coat, soccer clothes, or even lunch, the child will experience a temporary discomfort—but this is not the end of the world; instead it is a tangible learning experience. We don't need to be responsible for everything; we can incrementally hand responsibility to our kids and also allow their problems to stay in their lap.

Wilderness therapy and Buddhist philosophy have taught me very simple approaches to the complicated problem of parenting today. Less is more—this is the path of brave parenting. Let's let our kids tackle their own problems. Let's step out of the current and rest on the bank of the river. We are not abandoning them, and we are not ignoring them—we are nearby, but we're just not inserting ourselves into their tumult. Our kids will never become resourceful or resilient when we solve everything.

This is not to say we cannot help. We can offer advice—if it is asked for. We can provide loving support. We can set boundaries and enforce rules, and we can offer positive reinforcement. And we can (and sometimes should) consult with professionals.

The practices in this book are not suggested as a substitute for medical or psychological care or advice. Always seek the advice of a physician or other qualified health provider with any questions you may have regarding a medical condition. Never disregard professional medical advice or delay in seeking it because of something you have read here.

This is a book for all parents—single, together or apart, heterosexual or LGBTQ—with children of any age. Obviously, setting healthy patterns is most effective when children are young; however, these concepts can be successfully applied at birth, age five, age fifteen, and beyond. I work with many parents who have struggling college-age children; the parenting approaches presented in this book can be adapted and implemented at any point in the parent-child life cycle.

The ideas in this book are both for children who appear to be following the more "normal" path of development *and* children who are struggling emotionally or behaviorally. Building moccasins is a lifelong process for all of us. These concepts foster healthy parent-child patterns whether applied once your child starts talking or after he or she starts giving you the silent treatment.

This book is about creating moccasins to enable our kids to mature and individuate. With the skills presented in this book, you will equip them to navigate their own life trails.

Krissy

INTRODUCTION
Moccasins

Shantideva was an eighth-century Indian monk who was born a prince but renounced the throne to follow the path of the Buddha. His wisdom, particularly the quote used in the epigraph of this book, remains relevant in our age of anxiety. In this excerpt, Shantideva said, in essence: When you walk on the earth your feet may get cut. He illuminates metaphorically how, in an attempt to control our life situations, we lay down leather wherever we step so we don't hurt our feet; we try to gain control over our external environments. We think if we have more control, more security, we will feel less anxious about the unknowns in life. Yet, as Shantideva points out, this as a futile process because we cannot lay hides of leather to cover all of the earth. Instead, we can simply wrap leather around our feet.

Most of us endlessly focus on ordering ours and our children's immediate environments to avoid experiencing any discomfort. We are perpetually warding off pain and trying to keep unease at bay. This is understandable, yet problematic. Attempting to control our environments not only limits our lives—it creates a false reality, as most things in life cannot be controlled. Mother Nature reminds us of this fact, with hurricanes, earthquakes, and fires. We're also subject to the buffeting winds of financial collapses, terrorism, bullying, school shootings, family or health problems, and illness or death—nothing is completely secure.

Fearing that things may go wrong, however, does keep anxiety and tension in our lives, which wall us off from direct experiences in the present moment. Most of us are "on guard" in our lives—especially as parents—yet these barriers prevent us from experiencing moments in our lives and moments with our children: a beaming smile or a meltdown, a success or a failure.

This trap of "control" heightens when we have children. In childrearing today, we try to create the perfect environment for our kids, from the "right" baby gear, foods, and toys, to the "right" friends, school, teacher, sports, and clothes, so our kids will not experience any suffering—and in turn we as parents will not feel any pain. We are endlessly vigilant, trying to make our kids happy, boost their self-esteem, and help them experience success.

Yet in our attempts to find control, we are actually putting our kids at a disadvantage, because their little feet are still exposed to the sharp rocks at the edge of the leather—rocks that they don't know how to navigate. And as hard as we try to steer and guide them, we cannot control where they step. When we keep laying down leather, we are increasing the emotional vulnerability of our kids, since they are used to us fixing all their discomforts. This is a disempowering pattern and interferes with their ability to be emotionally resilient.

Many of you may be thinking, "Well, Krissy, there are real threats out there. What are we supposed to do, nothing?" Of course not. We actually want our children to face what I call "safe struggle": daily struggle in the home and school, struggle that we can frame as a problem that we ask our children to solve, rather than anticipating it, fixing it, and smoothing it over. Homework issues, sibling conflict, friendship tensions, upsets over household or school rules, chore frustrations, and parent-child conflicts can all be valued and highlighted as perfect material for moccasin building. We don't need to hover over and manage and fix everything. We can compassionately leave these problems in our children's laps. When kids can navigate safe struggle they are more likely to have skills when they face more real threats outside the home, such as rejection from a boyfriend, peer pressure, or some sort of failure or setback.

This is the rich fertile soil of the home where kids can develop what I call internal resources to navigate their life trail; we can create a home environment that fosters the moccasin-building process by framing struggle positively. These internal resources that children can learn in the home include delayed gratification, problem solving, adaptability, emotional regulation, distress tolerance, internal motivation, and self-discipline. I should note that these internal resources are hardly recognizable in our on-demand, overinvolved, and electronically tethered parenting culture.

Valuing struggle is counterintuitive but important. As our Western society advances in science, technology, and medicine it may seem as though we are improving the human experience, but concurrently Westerners are becoming less adaptable to change, less resilient, and more vulnerable to mental health struggles. As a society we continue to run from discomfort, conflicts, and problems. We are always reaching out for something external to take away the pain—a pill, a video, an escape, a distraction, or a bed to fall into—rather than employing the age-old techniques of staying, persevering, and even maturing as result of discomfort or hardship. We have survived adversity for millennia; these abilities are in our genes, yet we don't ask our children to use them.

Somewhere along the line, the perception of children has swung from sturdy to fragile, so delicate that they need constant protection and surveillance. Parents work hard to remove obstacles and mitigate struggles in their children's lives so as not to upset their tenuous, emerging sense of selves. This books lays out a radically different paradigm: using negative experiences and struggles as the means to promote internal resource development and emotional maturation in young people. Rather than having their hurdles removed by their parents, children can master their own life obstacles. Our children may have a disability or may encounter loss, but they may also be able to minimize or even avoid the emotional upheaval and mental anguish (panic, depression, despair, insomnia, anger, anxiety) associated with these obstacles. When kids master one obstacle, they are more prepared for the next boulder along their path.

As Shantideva says, instead of controlling our environment, we can work with our minds, so we can be in any life situation and have the ability to stay present rather than look for an exit. Likewise, we can teach our children to stay present in their life challenges.

Subclinical Behaviors

I have found that many parents today would rather their child have a concrete diagnosis, such as an anxiety or learning disorder for which there might be a specialist or treatment, rather than an assessment that their child simply has poor internal resources and coping abilities. Some call this "medicalizing" children's behaviors. Although this isn't rational, it fits with the parental reflex of placing responsibility outside our children.

When a child receives a diagnosis, some parents even use these labels to further comfort and rescue their children. "Well, he has ADHD, so he needs to have me help him with his homework every night" or "She does not know how to manage her anger, so I just have to absorb it and adjust" or "Boredom triggers his anxiety, so I have to keep him on a schedule." The parents' efforts to "manage" their children shift into a higher gear. With or without a label or diagnosis, parents today tiptoe around their children's moods and behaviors. Why are we so afraid of holding children accountable for inappropriate behavior?

Moreover, cultivating our children's internal strengths is largely missing from our childrearing discourse. Words like *bravery, resourcefulness,* and *adaptability* are absent from current treatment and mental health vocabularies. Resiliency is more viewed as an inborn capacity that some lucky children have rather than something that can be fostered. Today we baby our children—we largely treat them as younger than their biological age.

Many kids who show up in therapists' and learning specialists' offices don't fall into clear diagnoses. These children exhibit what are called "subclinical behaviors" that parents don't know how to deal with. For example: kids giving up and acting helpless, kids with iron-willed stubbornness, sneaky and deceptive kids, irritable kids with anger outbursts, kids who shut down and stonewall their parents, savvy bright kids who work their parents in circles, skilled negotiators, and emotional exaggerators. Some kids cycle through a mixture of these behaviors.

There are of course children who have clear mental health diagnoses or learning disabilities, not just poor coping skills. In such cases, these types of subclinical behaviors are also frequently exhibited, mixed in with their disorders, impeding professionals and complicating the treatment process.

Many of the children who display these behaviors are stuck in problematic patterns of behavior that play out in the parent-child relationship. It should also be noted that all of these behaviors produce some desirable outcome for the child: a rule changing, a parent's giving in, a removal of a chore, or simply the triggering of a parent's emotional reaction, which can feel powerful to a child. At a minimum these behaviors certainly get their parent's attention. With these subclinical behaviors, kids are gaining dominance in the home environment, rather than adapting internally and maturing—and they've become dependent on the leather being there to cushion them.

Why Moccasins?

Many young people today are lacking in internal resources, adaptability, and resilience. Kids panic when they experience discomfort and run straight to Mom or Dad, as if parents have the tools to fix everything. (It should be noted that many parents enjoy and endorse this process, labeling it as "closeness" in the parent-child relationship.) Parents think that it's their responsibility to always make sure their child is happy. But when parents start out thinking they can solve all their children's problems, inevitably they run into trouble—eventually the child will want the parents to fix something that is truly out of their domain. It's best to let kids learn to problem-solve small struggles and discomforts in their life, ideally when they are young, before they experience their first social rejection or their first academic, athletic, or artistic defeat.

We are all oriented toward happiness, yet happiness is not the issue. We think that happiness is something that should be there all the time; if it is not, then something is wrong. In reality happiness comes and goes. We need to step away from the notion of constant happiness and move toward a concept of emotional heath.

Instead of focusing all of our attention and research on happiness, we need to learn how to just be with sadness, disappointment, worry, anger, embarrassment, struggle, failure, until these feelings subside. If we are comfortable enough with all emotions and can experience them without reactivity, chances are we will be emotionally healthy. This is why we need to let children get to know all their feelings.

Buddhism teaches that *anicca*, or impermanence, is a characteristic of all things. Ultimately, impermanence is our friend; it allows sadness, pain, and disappointment to fade into new emotional states. When we process emotions naturally, they are fluid. Impermanence keeps us present and on our toes—life is always shifting, changing, and new.

This book uses metaphors tried and tested on kids and parents, as well as gleaned from my years in wilderness therapy, from parent coaching, from my own experiences as a parent, and from my study of Buddhism. Kids relate to metaphors more easily than complicated feelings.

"Moccasins" is the metaphor I use for internal resources. Moccasins get us from point A to point B, whether we are walking in our house, through school, or up Mount Everest. They are the skill set to navigate our emotional terrain.

The internal resources I am describing in this book are the following:

▶ **Delayed gratification:** An ability to work toward something without an immediate reward.
▶ **Problem solving:** An ability to move from a given state toward a more desired goal.
▶ **Adaptability:** An ability to cope with an unexpected disturbance.
▶ **Emotional regulation:** An ability to shift into and out of different feeling states or behaviors.
▶ **Distress tolerance:** An ability to stay with discomfort.
▶ **Internal motivation:** An internal (as opposed to external) locus of control that drives behavior.
▶ **Self-discipline:** An ability to motivate oneself, regardless of emotional state.
▶ **Acceptance of impermanence:** An awareness that nothing lasts forever.

In *The Way of the Bodhisattva*, Shantideva says, "We should guard our minds with the same care with which we would protect a broken or wounded arm while moving through an unruly crowd." These internal resources are the tools that will guard our minds and emotional states; the unruly crowd is the vicissitudes of life. When we can tolerate distress, emotionally regulate ourselves, motivate ourselves without immediate gratification, adapt to disturbances, and recognize that change is constant, we will be able to maintain a more resilient, stable, and open mind. Buddhists have been working with the mind for millennia; it is now time to bring these concepts into modern parenting.

Without moccasins, kids are exposed to grave threats such as delayed maturity, mental health struggles, recklessness, impulsivity, and self-destructive behaviors—despite their parents' hovering ways—because they do not know how to self-manage and adapt to the shifting landscape of life. We must instead encourage them to experience their own emotions, face their own obstacles, and build their internal resources. We can communicate to our children and instill in them that each of them has his or her own innate ability to problem-solve—it just needs to be honed and developed. If we want our kids to have inner strength, we have to help cultivate it. Our message can be "You've got this," rather than "I'll fix it."

How Do Kids Make Their Moccasins?

With the current breakdown in societal supports such as religious institutions, community programs, and strong schools, kids aren't navigating independently outside the home as they did in previous generations. At the same time, kids have more free rein inside the home—with both parents often working and usually without live-in relatives. Additionally, children have more access to the adult world through television, the internet, video games, and so on. Yet kids don't have the skills to manage all this. The home has become a place of comfort, a place to check out, not a place to be accountable. However, the home is *also* the perfect environment for moccasin building.

How do we teach children to accept discomfort and uncertainty? How do we teach kids to feel their emotions and not run away from them—to know that struggle is a normal part of development? As parents, we need to work on accepting our own and try to normalize and contextualize rather than fix our children's. We need to do so ourselves and also validate our children's emotional experiences. How do we help cultivate their abilities to problem-solve, to stay with problems so they can manage their own rocks and boulders? We need to not panic when we face our own obstacles, and we need to value their problem-solving skills.

Adversity is part of the human experience, not something to attempt to remove at every turn. Discomfort can actually be a gift in disguise that helps us build inner strength. We can instill in our children that we are okay if they fall because we trust them to get up on their own—to repair and mend their moccasins.

How Can Parents Help?

Let's face it; parents are already overinvolved. How can parents' involvement and attention shift away from laying down the leather and toward moccasin building?

Rather than hovering over our little seedlings, constantly watching and monitoring their growth and development, trying to give them the perfect amount of sun, shade, and water—we can instead keep feeding the soil. The soil is the nurturing ground of the home. We can't control the storms that are coming, we can't control the genetics in the seeds, but we can cultivate rich, fertile soil. We can do this by role modeling healthy emotional management, validating feelings, valuing safe struggle, refraining from rescuing, setting proper boundaries and limits, teaching problem solving and accountability, giving natural and logical consequences, and accepting impermanence in life.

The Structure of This Book

The following chapters teach the moccasin-building process by using a variety of nature-based metaphors and stories that teach parents how to navigate the murky landscape of childrearing. Parenting techniques that help foster the internal resources I've listed above will be further elaborated in the coming chapters. Loving our kids is the easy part—dealing with their emotions and behaviors is not so easy.

This book is divided into four parts. Part 1 is focused on emotions. Part 2 is focused on behaviors. Part 3 discusses obstacles that parents and children encounter. Part 4 describes a new closeness that parents and their children can forge—two trails, side by side. In each part there are three chapters: the first chapter is devoted to everyday parenting; the second chapter places more emphasis on children struggling with different emotional or behavioral patterns; the third chapter highlights specific skills to apply in your parenting today.

In many of these chapters I illustrate my points with examples of children and their parents. While these anecdotes are drawn from my experiences as a therapist, names, ages, genders, and various details of the stories have been changed, so the people in the stories should be viewed as fictional.

When we model how to sew and repair our moccasins, our children will learn how to make and mend their own. We can stay present with their feelings without fixing them. We can let them experience consequences, let them solve problems on their own. With moccasins, when our kids experience obstacles in life, they will be better able to navigate them. We need to give our children the freedom of having their own life, not one managed by us. We need to be brave and trust that life will hand them the lessons they need. We can then empower them to travel where they want and explore their own terrain, because we have faith that they will have the inner resources, emotional resilence, and guidance to get there.

PART I

The River:
The Course of Emotions

CHAPTER 1
Letting Your Kids Feel

At an emotional level, we feel that things should be happy and when things are difficult or painful, something is wrong. According to the Buddhist teachings this is what causes suffering.

—Pema Chodron

Willow

"I am not going to go on a walk to the playground without Doggie!" exclaimed five-year-old Willow, referring to the rather large stuffed animal that she sleeps with.

"Sweetie, you know I am going to end up carrying her the whole time, or she's going to be left on the ground near the swings and get all dirty. Let's just put your doggie in your bed for a nap," her father replied.

As they started walking out the door, Willow dragged her big doggie out onto the driveway. Her dad pleaded, "Sweetie, I said we're not going to bring Doggie; I'm going to go in and put her on your bed."

Willow sat down on the grass and wailed, "I am not going without Doggie!"

Feeling frustrated and anxious to get on with the day, her dad grabbed Doggie. Off they went on their walk, four blocks to the playground.

At the playground Willow instantly took off her shoes and began skipping around and humming a song. Her dad felt a tightening in his chest. He was uncomfortable and worried that there might be glass or other sharp objects at a public playground but wanted to avoid another struggle; he decided to temporarily overlook it. He saw that she was happy. He went down the slide with her, pushed her in the swing, and then chased her around the playground. Doggie sat on the bench by the park.

Over by the sandbox, Willow yelled, "Hey, Daddy, come here!" She was sneakily hiding something in her hands behind her back. As her dad approached, she surprised him by throwing sand right at his face and chest. Though dismayed by this act, Dad quickly collected himself and said, "Sweetie, you can throw sand at my back but not my front, as it may get in my eyes." He turned around and showed her his back. She began heaving sand at his back like a vicious sandstorm. After enough activity, Dad retrieved Doggie, and he and Willow sang songs on their way home for lunch.

Accepting Our Emotions

Parenting today has shifted toward children's emotions and away from children's behavior. We are culturally very concerned with their happiness and, more importantly, with having a close parent-child bond. Yet I would argue that in fact we are not comfortable enough with emotions—our children's or our own. As you can see, Willow's father denied his feelings of frustration, worry, and discomfort and worked hard to protect his daughter from feeling any negative emotion. We have very little tolerance for our children's feelings of sadness or disappointment—we are only comfortable with our children feeling happy. But what message does this send—that it's only okay for children to feel one emotion?

Yet we all *still* experience a range of emotions every day. Our resisting, warding off, or actively fighting unpleasant feelings is why we are stressed. We all do this. We don't want to feel such things, so we expend lot of energy in dulling, numbing, projecting, displacing, avoiding, distracting, acting out these unwanted feelings, or wanting others to rescue us from them. What would happen to our stress if we allowed ourselves to accept and feel our emotions—even if they included pain, sadness, or worry? What would happen if we listened to our feelings as important information, which we could use to guide our decisions? What would happen if we did not judge our emotions and, in turn, ourselves?

We all have emotions. Not just happy, sad, mad, but a full spectrum: dread, elation, panic, thrill, ease, restlessness, fear, embarrassment, rage, wonder, and contentment. Emotions are like music or colors. Music would not be as vibrant or penetrating without the full spectrum of sounds—light and ethereal, as well as dark and foreboding. Similarly, each shade of the color palette is critical to the delicate beauty that exists in nature and art. We don't value yellow as good and grey as bad, or a high musical note as good and a low note as bad; they are all vital.

The emotional spectrum creates the texture of the human experience. Let's face it: despite the energy we spend evading worry, depression, and hurt, life would be pretty dull without such feelings. They are central and integral to experiencing a rich and satisfying life. Nobody lives a pain-free life. The trick is to learn to accept and experience all feelings, to see them as important information, rather than exaggerate them through creating drama or shut them down through a control mechanism. It is such a relief when someone reassuringly lets us feel without fixing: "It is okay to be negative." "It's natural to feel worried." "That is painful." "I imagine that's frustrating."

Furthermore, what if emotions are so important that they are the key to really knowing ourselves? Sadness is an indicator of a loss; this is something every human knows, because everyone experiences loss. Guilt is connected to caring about whether we harm others or ourselves. Our bodies are designed to feel anxiety if we think a threat is on the horizon or a large emotional shift is about to happen, like a move, a job change, a new baby, a graduation, or a marriage. Anger can be a sign that we need to change something in our lives, make our feelings known, or simply to tell someone "no." What if emotions give us critical information every day about how to live or how to parent? What if negative emotions are just as or even more important than positive emotions in giving us guidance in our lives?

The problem is we don't value our emotional input, and we judge ourselves when we feel anything but happy. Most of us do not know how to successfully be with negative emotions since our whole lives we have been told "Don't worry," "It's okay," "Cheer up," "Feel better," and even "It's not that big of a deal" and "Stop crying." This sends the strong cultural message that if you feel a negative emotion, something about you must be wrong and you need to get rid of the emotion quickly.

How Do We Sit and Stay with Our Emotions?

I learned to work with emotions in two places: in my career in wilderness therapy and through Buddhism. Although they are very different disciplines, they share core concepts.

In wilderness therapy, emotions are viewed just as they are. There are no labels or projections of good or bad, right or wrong. Though kids in wilderness settings still have their own idiosyncratic way of amplifying feelings—such as yelling, posturing, or giving up—at a core place the message is that there is nothing wrong with feeling "negative" emotions in and of themselves. What becomes clear in the wilderness is that the problem is the behavior—not the emotion. When kids feel anger, it is validated; when kids show disrespect and defiance, there are consequences. The essential distinction is this: all feelings are accepted and all behaviors must be accounted for. In the wilderness, this becomes straightforward.

Furthermore, in wilderness therapy, the coping mechanisms that are used in day-to-day life to manage one's emotions may not exist. There are no doors to slam, televisions to escape to, computer games to play, cell phones to gossip on, or junk food or other addictions to indulge in. There is nothing for kids to reach for in order to numb themselves. Of course there are still mental layers of defense—such as closing-off, denial, lying, or sarcasm—but they break down when the child spends time in a raw and exposed landscape. Without escape mechanisms, the greatest lesson of wilderness therapy is how to sit with your feelings. Emotions begin to be experienced in an unadulterated way, which is refreshing and new to most kids. This opening up and validation of feelings is also socially endorsed through daily groups.

When adolescents in the wilderness experience their feelings, they notice that they eventually pass. In fact, research shows that the life span of an emotion lasts three to thirty minutes—if we let it be. Of course an emotion can also last three days, if we really go to work fighting it. We *think* we can control or delete unwanted feelings. In the wilderness we must soften to the idea that there are things we can't control; this comes with the realities of living in the natural world.

In the wilderness the laws of nature determine everything. When it is cold, our efforts are toward getting warm. When it is hot, efforts are placed on finding shade and cool water. The natural world imparts lessons. When it is cold, we don't deny reality and say, "Don't feel cold, feel warm." Instead the cold informs and motivates us to put on a coat and mittens and to begin to collect firewood. This does not change the cold; instead, there is sense of abiding, accepting, and working with the cold. When it is windy, we realize there's no point in saying, "Oh, wind, stop; I want sun." We know we can't stop the wind, so we have to feel it. Even if we find some shelter, we can still hear the wind and feel it blowing through the tent. There is no escaping; the wilderness forces you to stay with the present moment.

Yet when we stay with these textures of life, both pleasant and unpleasant, we notice that they pass. In fact, if we really feel the cold, and really feel the wind, chances are the next time it is sunny, we are going to make sure we feel and notice and experience that sun and appreciate its warmth—this is joy.

We know we cannot control or change the weather, so we accept it. What would happen if we also realized that we cannot change or control our feelings—only our behaviors? What if we allowed ourselves to see sadness or anxiety like the rain; rather than trying to control it, we can let it pour over us until it clears up?

There is a great poem by Rilke on this subject:

> Let everything happen to you: beauty and terror.
> Just keep going. No feeling is final

No feeling is final; everything passes.

There are clear similarities in the underlying concepts of wilderness therapy and the teachings of Buddhism. Buddhists, knowing that life is constantly in flux, talk about having a "stable mind." This concept of stability is not viewed through the lens of mental illness but rather through the lens of the human experience. For example, most of us have mental states that rise and fall based on daily events that we perceive as good or bad: a hug and a smile from your daughter (good!), getting stuck in construction traffic and being late for a meeting (bad). Buddhism encourages you to meet all events with equanimity.

A core premise of Buddhism is impermanence—*anicca*. Life and all things are in constant motion; the only certainty is that each day we are all taking a step closer to our deaths. When all things are "secure" and in place, this is sort of like a death, because it is contrary to the ebb and flow of life. For example, we all know the irritation when you mow your lawn, pay your bills, and clean your house and think everything is in place—then the dishwasher breaks or your muddy dog tramps through the house. Yet this is the nature of things, up and down. We suffer when we fight this ebb and flow. We always want life to stay still or to improve. We want to feel pleasure and avoid pain. We want profits every quarter. Yet as much as we pretend we aren't, we are part of nature and we are not in control.

Because of the uncertainty of every part of life, an underlying anxiety always exists. Anxiety is not a sign that something is wrong with us; it is an experience of being alive in an impermanent world. So, for example, this is not a feeling we can "fix" for our kids. Anxiety is a normal emotion that every human feels, and our suffering around it dissipates when we acknowledge and accept it. When we fight anxiety is when we experience stress.

With this perspective of impermanence, Buddhist teachers encourage us to pay attention to life's fluctuations as a simple coming and going; they don't put a lot of value on events as good and bad, focusing instead on noticing what is. Just like in wilderness therapy, Buddhism recognizes emotions for what they are: messengers with information about the moment we are in.

These teachings and perspectives are particularly poignant in the face of the modern world's catastrophes: collapsing financial systems, hurricanes, terrorism, tsunamis, earthquakes, and school shootings. Even the best medicine or insurance can't create complete security. Our children are bound to experience sadness, pain, despair, confusion, and uncertainty.

Just as we do in wilderness therapy, in Buddhist meditation we remove all external stimuli, all outward escape patterns, and begin to work with our minds. No matter how your mind skips around—fantasizing about your next vacation, rehashing your last argument, or experiencing peace and dread—in meditation you focus on *coming back to the breath*. Our breath creates an anchor and stability in the ups and downs of life. When we can feel alive through our breath we can more reliably stay with our delight *and* discomfort.

When we accept our sadness or our worry and really experience it, it is likely that we will fully appreciate our next laugh. Rather than staying on guard and skimming the surface of life—we can accept, allow, and go *toward* the textures of life. Life would not be very interesting if we only had sunny days, bright colors, happy music, and uplifting emotions. If we trust that it will ebb and flow, we don't have to get too caught up in one emotion. Tibetan Buddhist teacher Pema Chodron calls this "no big deal." In fact what gets us stuck is resisting a feeling or a moment—this disrupts the natural fluctuations. This in turn causes us stress.

It is important to note that staying with emotions is not as simple as I may be explaining it—because we all start out as children, and we learn about emotions from parents and other adults. These messages of escaping unwanted emotions are imprinted on us since our birth. We then, of course, pass them on to our children: "Cheer up, sweetie." "It's okay." "Don't worry about it." "You'll be fine." "I'll fix it." "There is nothing to be mad about." Though parents mean well, so many statements about emotions are invalidating. This is quite confusing for little ones.

To further complicate matters, when parents have a child with some mental health or behavioral struggles, parents are even more afraid to validate a negative emotion, lest their child become more inclined toward depression or anxiety. Parents worry: "He might think anger is okay." "She might become sad all the time." "I don't want him to feel anxiety; I have to try to help fix it." Yet is it critical for parents to again see that all these concerns are rooted in fear. We can't control our children's emotions, but we can control our reactions and responses. Even if we feel anxious, we can stay with it and feel the adrenalin pumping through us—which means we love our kids and want to take their pain away.

Knowing that emotions rise up and fall away, kids can learn to process their emotions in the most natural way, which is staying present and experiencing them until they pass. Just like strong trees endure all the seasons, kids can stay with their spectrum of emotions. This is the texture of life; this enhances kids' emotional resilience, their ability to build their own moccasins.

Normalizing and Validating Kids' Experiences

When one of my daughters was six, she said, "My face looks weird."

I felt a strong impulse to say, "What do you mean? Your face is beautiful." But I knew this was sidestepping whatever her concern was, and I also knew that it is an entirely normal process to examine our appearances—it's part of coming to grips with who we are. At a certain age we all become aware of mirrors and what we see in the mirror when we look in.

I refrained from my preprogrammed parental response and decided to become curious. I know I cannot (and should not) take her self-discovery process away from her, but I can validate and normalize the process. So I said, "What do you mean?" She said, "Well, in pictures, and in the mirror—I think my face looks funny." So I said, "Do you think my face looks weird?" "No," she replied. Then I asked, "What do you think of your father? Does his face look weird?" "No," she replied. Then both my husband and I reinforced and validated that we remember having similar feelings as kids, and even still think we look strange at times. After we validated her concern, I offered my insight: "I also think you're just not used to looking at your own face all day long, like you're used to looking at ours." (I realize that adding this may have been my attempt to "rescue" her from her feelings.)

Rather than disputing her thoughts and feelings, we earnestly tried to validate what I imagine to be a fairly normal human experience of looking into a mirror. Validation is an enormous relief to kids—to hear the truth and to know they are not alone in their feelings.

Older kids might make more extreme statements about their life or self: "I am ugly." "I hate myself." "I am stupid." Even these are fruitless to oppose, as damaging as they may seem, because at their roots are emotions. The root emotion is what parents should try to discover and address, rather than simply respond with a compliment. Though parents have the best of intentions when they say "You're so pretty" or "You're such a great kid" or "You're so smart," over time these statements come up short. In fact kids feel can worse when they're praised, because not only do they still feel bad about themselves, but they also feel guilty or wrong for feeling that way, because we tell them that they are fine. I call this the "double negative." This is where stress comes in.

Double and Triple Negatives

Stress develops not only when we are anxious and overwhelmed but also when we judge and resist the fact that we are anxious and overwhelmed. This double negative inclines us to reach for a negative coping pattern to feel better, which unfortunately causes what I call a "triple negative."

A Kid's Negative Pattern

Single Negative: Worry about a confusing math assignment.

Double Negative: Stress from your mom's attempts to cheer you up—which makes you feel worse because Mom says the assignment's not hard.

Triple Negative (Behavior Pattern): Yelling at your mom, slamming the door in her face, and feeling angry all night.

A Parent's Negative Pattern

Single Negative: Sadness and worry that your child is being rejected by a friend at school.

Double Negative: Rather than staying with the feeling, you attempt to control it through lecturing and suggesting ideas about how to be a friend.

Triple Negative (Behavior Pattern): When your child doesn't listen, you scold the child and take a victim stance, feeling like he or she never appreciates you.

For some there is even a fourth negative: a denial of the behavioral pattern, during which neither the adults nor the children take accountability for their acting out. When there is a fourth negative it is like pressing the repeat button for this pattern to happen over and over again. When we don't allow our selves or our kids to experience primary emotions like sadness, disappointment, worry, or frustration, we unfortunately keep piling on layers of negatives. Pretty soon the whole home becomes negative. How can we reverse this and let our children (and our selves) feel? How do we stay at one negative?

Letting Kids Feel

In my example with my daughter, she did not sound upset, just concerned, so I mirrored back concern. But when kids make more emotionally charged statements, it is even more important for parents to stay with the emotions. Frequently parents respond to children's emotionality with rationality, and this most likely results in another power struggle or dead end.

Here are the steps to letting kids feel, which you could also call *mirroring*, *validation*, *normalizing*, or *reflective listening*:

1) Identify and focus on your child's emotion, rather than the content of the concern.
2) Reflect the feelings back to your child.
3) Become curious.
4) Validate your child's feelings.
5) Let your child be in charge of solving the problem—this is where kids become empowered and feel a sense of mastery in their own lives.
6) Keep your own opinions out of your child's problem. The only time to bring yourself in is for validation purposes: "I get frustrated by that as well." Only bring in your own opinion if your child specifically asks: "Mom, what do you think?"

In these three scenarios, the parent did not change, invalidate, or attempt to take away the child's thought, emotion, or problem. When parents refute their children's emotional statements with "You are smart and pretty," this never makes a child feel better, because it skips a child's core concern. However, parents can steer away from distorted thoughts by highlighting and validating underlying emotions, which encourages the child's emotional river to flow. This process also encourages problem solving and moccasin building.

Example 1

Son: "I hate myself."

Mom, mirroring: "You sound so upset."

Son: "I am miserable."

Mom, becoming curious: "Did something happen?"

Son: "I just mess assignments up all the time, and I handed the wrong one in. I'm an idiot."

Mom, validating: "That sounds frustrating."

Son: "It is!"

Mom: "Do you want to talk about it?"

Son: "Not really."

Mom, letting her child be in charge of the problem: "What do you think you will do?"

Son: "I don't know. I guess I'll have to redo my assignment."

Mom, validating by including herself: "I hate when that happens."

Son: "Yeah, I know."

The mom did not insert herself into the problem nor oppose her son, and as a result she stayed on his side.

Example 2

Daughter: "I'm so stupid."

Dad, mirroring: "You sound upset."

Daughter: "I am!"

Dad, becoming curious: "What happened?"

Daughter: "I'm never going to understand math."

Dad, validating: "That must be upsetting to feel."

Daughter: "It is."

Dad refrains from jumping in.

Daughter: "Do you think you can help me tonight?"

Dad, letting his daughter be in charge: "Okay, that sounds good. What do you think you need help with?"

Daughter: "I need help understanding the first few, because those are always confusing to me."

Dad, "Okay, tell me when you're ready."

Daughter: "Thanks, Dad."

Dad sidestepped her self-criticism and let her stay in charge, which is actually empowering and more validating than telling her she is smart.

Example 3

Daughter: "I'm so ugly."

Mom, mirroring: "Sweetie, you sound so upset."

Daughter: "I am; I'm repulsive."

Mom, becoming curious: "Did something happen?"

Daughter: "No. Well, yes, I guess. Jenny is now dating Eric. And it makes me feel like a loser. I don't look like *her*."

Mom, validating and asking questions: "That sounds frustrating... Did you like Eric?"

Daughter: "Sort of."

Mom: "What is he like?"

Daughter pauses: "I guess he's just a popular kid... I don't really know him, but he's cute."

Mom: "That sounds hard, sweetie. Is Jenny your friend?'

Daughter: "No, she's annoying."

Mom, letting her daughter stay in charge: "What do you think you'll do about it?"

Daughter: "Nothing, but can we rent a movie tonight?"

Mom: "Sure, that sounds good."

Mom listened but did not get involved. She allowed her daughter to have her own feelings and also allowed her determine what to do about it. In this case, watching a movie might help her relax a little; instead of using the movie as a way to fix a feeling, a movie can be a way for a mom and daughter to enjoy a night together.

When parents have a fear of any deficit or struggle in their child—whether it's that their child is not smart enough, pretty enough, athletic, or musical enough—parents may constantly fill in the fear with compliments and praise, like pouring water into a cup. However, no amount of reassurance will help if there's a hole in the child's cup. Rather than pouring compliments, time, money, or energy into making our kids feel happy, it's best to validate feelings and validate that struggle is a normal part of life. Struggle is not something to cover up or get rid of.

When kids feel seen and heard they move on; emotions and feelings pass. Parents should trust that their children will naturally shift on their own, when they are ready. Just like storm clouds move in and then move out—there is nothing to get alarmed about. This process allows negative emotional experiences to stay at one negative and not spiral into two, three, or even four. When parents feel they need to "fix" or intervene, this starts the layering of negatives.

How many times have you tried to make your child happy and had it backfire? Or, as in Willow's case, attempt to give your child what she wants, while noticing she never appreciates it and instead just keeps on pushing?

Working with Willow

I imagine some aspect of Willow's story will feel familiar to every parent. We often either give children what they want and feel frustrated that they don't appreciate it or agitated that we went back on our word, or we hold firm and our child escalates more, and then we get angry at our child or ourselves. We have to learn to listen to our own feelings as parents and communicate respectfully with our children.

Willow's dad, Jake, did not want to bring Doggie to the park. He had a variety of reasons, and as a dad he is allowed to set the rules and boundaries for his five-year-old daughter. Willow is allowed to feel sad and disappointed for not getting what she wants. This experience, of not getting what we want, is probably something that happens to every human on the planet at least once every day. We can't send the message to our kids that they can always get what they want, because we will always eventually come up against something we can't give them.

Instead we can mirror, attune, validate, and be present as parents when they feel upset.

Although Jake genuinely cares for his daughter and is not an abusive or neglectful parent, I believe these unhealthy parent-child patterns left unchecked can interfere with a child's ability to process emotions and problem-solve. In Jake's case, he is interrupting Willow's ability to feel upset, resolve the feeling, and move on, on her own.

When children leave their emotions at their parents' feet, asking their parents to fix their feelings, this leads to enmeshed parent-child patterns. When relationships become enmeshed neither the parent nor child is accountable for his or her own feelings. This can lead children and teens to feel helpless and angry, because they believe it is someone else's job to fix their problems. They are dependent on their parents to lay down the leather wherever they step.

What is most important is for children to learn to process their emotions naturally—without harming themselves or others. This *is* something we can work on in the home. Let's explore some ways Jake could let Willow feel.

"Sweetie, are you feeling frustrated because I said that you can't bring Doggie?" Jake asked, when he came outside and found Willow crying on the grass.

"You're a mean daddy," blamed Willow.

"Willow, you can say 'I feel mad at you, Daddy' or 'I feel frustrated at you, Daddy,' but you are not allowed to call me mean."

"I feel mad at you, Daddy," sulked Willow.

"Well, I hear that you feel mad at me. I accept your feeling. Thank you for telling me what you feel. We don't have to go to the park; it's up to you if you still want to go." Jake listened to his daughter and then gave her a choice, while holding his boundary.

Willow said she still wanted to go to the park. After they'd walked for a little bit, Willow began to skip; she felt her dad had heard her feelings, she'd processed them, and then she moved on. What kids want most is to be heard and accepted, not to always get their way.

At the park Willow began to take off her shoes. Jake reminded her that if she took off her shoes they would have to go back home, as she is not allowed to be barefoot at the playground. Willow listened and kept her shoes on. She continued to run around and play with him and she did not throw sand when they got to the sandbox. Jake was honoring his emotions and, with this, he was in touch with his own authority. Children naturally are more respectful to parents who express their authority authentically, rather than parents who are ambiguous or emotionally reactive.

When we let our children feel, we are letting them have their emotions, which include sadness and happiness. As a listener, you are letting your loved one stay with the feeling as long as is necessary, rather than rushing him or her out of it, changing it, or fixing it. This conveys acceptance. This is empathy. Chances are your child will move on after being heard; this cultivates the child's ability to emotionally regulate. This process also fosters healthy parent-child boundaries as well as closeness in the parent-child relationship, because both individuals' feelings are honored. The parent is not acquiescing to the whims of a child or betraying his or her own authority. This ability for a child to emotionally regulate is an essential tenet in building moccasins.

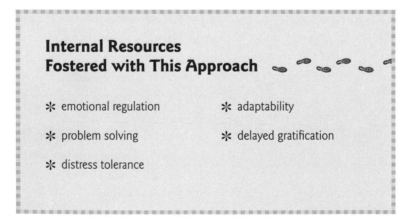

Internal Resources
Fostered with This Approach

* emotional regulation   * adaptability

* problem solving   * delayed gratification

* distress tolerance

CHAPTER 2

Removing the Dams in the River: Restoring Equilibrium

··

It has been a terrible, horrible, no good, very bad day.
My mom says some days are like that.
—Judith Viorst,
Alexander and the Terrible, Horrible, No Good, Very Bad Day

··

Our emotional life is like a river that courses through us; feelings, thoughts, and moods are constantly coming and going. This is natural. Sometimes an emotion gets stuck in an eddy, like sadness or negativity, and it takes over for a while until a piece of driftwood comes and pushes it back out into the current. Then a new thought, perspective, or feeling settles in. Emotions are moving and transient if we listen to them and let them be.

Emotions also bring information that can guide us. Worry about a busy day tomorrow might lead to planning tonight, anger or disappointment might lead to assertive communication or setting a limit, sadness about a sick friend might lead to making meals for her family. Other times there is nothing to do except accept our feelings: accept frustration when your flight is cancelled, accept disappointment when your child throws a temper tantrum and you are late to an important meeting, accept feeling overwhelmed when you are rushing through a chaotic day.

Sometimes, rather than being guided by a feeling, we go to war with it. We stop the river and fight the emotion in an attempt to control it because it is uncomfortable. These are the dams in our emotional river. When we oppose feelings we are actually keeping them stuck, which only builds more tension, tumult, and stress in our lives.

Insomnia

When I had a three-year-old and a seven-month-old, I went through a period of acute insomnia where I became intimate with the experience of fighting and damming emotions. I was so tired and had so much anxiety about being tired that I could not sleep. Being the mother of two small children only amplified my need for sleep, as well as my despair about not getting it. This further fueled many negative thoughts about my ability to parent. I remember feeling at the time that my life was like a logjam in a river—no water was moving because there were too many logs piled up, and I was stuck upstream, unfortunately awake.

One evening, a few months into my insomnia, my husband put the children to bed, and I went out to the local Buddhist meditation center to try to calm my anxious thoughts. As I was taking off my shoes before entering the meditation hall, I noticed a quote taped to the wall that said, "Chaos is very good news." This quote stopped me in my tracks. I was working very hard at the time trying to return order in my life, trying to sleep again. At that moment, I thought the quote was insane.

I was then surprised to see that the leader of the meditation group was my neighbor. I learned later that he is a Buddhist with thirty years of meditation under his belt—I soon connected the dots, realizing how open and present he always seemed. He was also surprised and delighted to see me join the group. He brought me into a side room to give me some simple instructions on sitting meditation. He explained, "The focus is just noticing the breath coming and going, in and out. When you get lost in thoughts, notice them and bring your attention back to the breath." I had done mediation before, in my twenties, but that had been focused on reciting mantras, not just breathing. Feeling fragile and on edge from my lack of sleep, I asked, "So what do we do with our thoughts?" (I wanted to say "our crazy, anxious thoughts," but didn't.) He replied, "Well, it's called *peaceful abiding*. You allow your thoughts to be there and gently bring your attention back to your breath, specifically your exhalation." Although I was still skeptical and wanted to learn exactly what *abiding* meant, I felt willing to try.

At this point, I'd explored medications, herbal remedies, yoga, lavender pillows, and a blue light by my bed, but studying these Buddhist concepts is what I can emphatically say cured my insomnia.

I had been trying desperately to get ground under my feet and was grasping for sleep. The definition of *abiding* is "to tolerate or endure," "to remain or to stay," and finally "to dwell." I hadn't been dwelling in the chaos of my life with young children; I was running from it. I was running from all the unknowns and uncertainties in an attempt to find order, and I was also busy fighting my anxious thoughts and tired feelings—no wonder I could not sleep.

In short, I dammed my river. As I was working hard to keep my anxiety and exhaustion at bay and working hard to have my life "together," I was also directly creating the tension and turmoil in my life. Only when I gave up *trying* to sleep, and abided with my fears, did I resume normal sleep patterns. Letting go of the hope of sleep and the fear of not sleeping, trusting in my body's innate ability to rest, trusting in my body's currents, I removed the dam. With deep acceptance, staying, and abiding, came sleep.

Though I would never wish insomnia on anyone, I can now say that it was truly a gift. I learned that we can embrace our life situations rather than fearing or trying to control them. When we remove the dams to the currents of our emotions, perhaps get the guidance of therapy, meditation, or other practices that bring clarity, we can restore harmony in our emotional lives. *Harmony* does not mean "happiness"; it means not going against the currents but instead abiding and accepting. How do we accept our circumstances and be with our emotions—however uncomfortable—so that they subside rather than escalate? How do we also accept our children's emotions and struggles rather than trying to fix or control?

Noah

Noah was a bright fourteen-year-old. He could think in complex, analytical ways; testing revealed that he had a very high IQ. He appeared to have a promising future, yet his ability to think through things could also trigger racing thoughts and paralyzing anxiety. He appeared to have some subtle obsessive-compulsive symptoms, such as meticulously straightening out his room and following a sequence of rituals before bed. Noah's two moms were both high-achieving individuals and were plagued with their own anxiety about their children finding and achieving success.

As Noah inched closer to middle school, he felt his parents turn up the volume on monitoring his homework, hyperfocusing on his grades, and repeatedly citing both the merits of high SAT scores and the competitiveness of college acceptance. Before he even reached high school he began to have stomachaches and headaches that kept him home from school, as well as other unexplained medical complaints.

With time, medical professionals began to believe that his ailments were psychological, but Noah refused to see a therapist. To cope with his restlessness and pervasive worry Noah began to find comfort in computer games, which channeled his intellect yet effectively distracted him from his underlying anxiety about life or schoolwork. This outlet created so much comfort for Noah that he found himself spending any spare moment on the computer and avoided relationships both at home and at school at all costs.

Noah's mothers were at a loss. They knew he had homework and study-skill issues that merited the need for a computer, yet it was hard to monitor how he was using the computer, especially when he said he was doing his homework. They also knew he had anxiety issues and did not want to engage in power struggles with him around rules, so they dropped household expectations and let him find comfort on the computer.

Both of Noah's parents worked, but soon monitoring Noah became a full-time job for his mother Sarah. She took a leave of absence from her job when Noah's anxiety grew debilitating. Sarah was constantly on alert for what he needed to do next, and she could never predict when he would follow through with tasks or when he would get stuck. This involved practically twenty-four-hour surveillance.

Yet Noah's parents were also constantly tiptoeing around his moods to avoid setting off his OCD and anxiety rituals. They did not know how to navigate the home and keep him accountable. Eventually Noah's grades slid so much that he began to receive bad grades: Cs, Ds, and even an F. Their bright son was failing ninth grade. He had effectively avoided and given up on school. In some ways, his parents felt like failures too.

Deep Acceptance of Your Children Who May Be Getting Stuck

When our children are really struggling with a behavioral, emotional, or learning issue, so often we don't want to see what is right in front of us. In fact, we find many ways to distort a truth that is just too uncomfortable to acknowledge. Many parents simply work harder and harder to keep their child on track. But if we clearly see what is there and then accept what is there—this is when real shifts happen.

The first time a parent might have one of these "aha!" moments is when their child pushes up against some behavioral limit and receives a diagnosis. Another might be when parents receive the results of their son or daughter's academic testing or psychological evaluation. Or perhaps it is when their child is advised to start a course of psychotropic medication. These are huge, seismic shifts that may be welcomed—to address a stubborn behavioral situation at home or school—or feared. Yet many of these reports and evaluations highlight features or patterns that a child may have exhibited for years perhaps his or her whole life. It's common for parents to shield themselves from these painful truths—and it is remarkable how many parents engage in magical thinking.

For example, if a child has started therapy or a treatment program, parents jump to a linear thought process: treatment = success in school = graduation = college = job = successful life. Parents swiftly want to get back on course. This is understandable. But with these blinders on, parents are trying to keep the pain at bay by erecting dams and resisting their currents. Parents *can* continue to have dreams and wishes for their child, but it is best to keep those goals much further out of view and stay in the present moment—however uncertain it may be.

For many parents, nothing in their child's life has followed a sequential or logical path. This is reality. Part of getting better (for both the child and the parents) is seeing the problem in a naked way—and even *letting* it break your heart. Remember, we need to accept the river of feelings that are there—and allow these emotions to take their natural course. Parents are sad, scared, and overwhelmed; it is best to actually feel those things. When parents model that they are afraid to feel and then engage in anxious behaviors like fixing, they are not opening themselves up and learning from the crisis; instead they are running from it.

It's okay to be brokenhearted—it means you love your child. Once parents mourn the loss of the life they wished for their child, they can accept and meet their child where he or she is today. For some this means giving up being a soccer mom or a hockey dad, relinquishing the dream of getting your daughter ready for the prom or dropping her off at her first-choice college, or even simply missing the events that populate the "normal" course through childhood. When parents continue to grasp tightly to what could have been (consciously or unconsciously), there will always be a hint of disappointment, which children notice. When parents fully feel this loss, they can fully accept who their child is and the gifts that a nontraditional path through childhood brings.

Tibetan Buddhist teacher Pema Chodron writes in *When Things Fall Apart* that giving up hope is "the beginning of the beginning. Without giving up hope—that there's somewhere better to be, that there's some-one better to be—we will never relax with where we are or who we are." Moreover, hope is always connected to fear; we hope that our struggling child will get better, but we fear that he or she won't. Pema writes: "The word in Tibetan for hope is *rewa*; the word for fear is *dokpa*. More commonly, the word *re-dok* is used, which combines the two. Hope and fear is a feeling with two sides. As long as there's one, there's always the other. This *re-dok* is the root of our pain."

This is the core of mindfulness: Staying present and experiencing this moment—no matter how painful it may be. If you can do this, chances are you will also be present when pain subsides into another emotion. Mark Epstein, a Buddhist psychotherapist, writes: "It is my experience that emotions, no matter how powerful, are not overwhelming if given room to breathe."

When parents let go of hope, as strange as this may sound, they are allowing themselves to feel this moment, this event. Rather than having your emotions caught up in your chest or throat, frozen in time, parents can let the river of feelings flow again—perhaps sleep again, smile again, even laugh again—despite whatever behavior their child is engaging in. This is acceptance. Epstein writes: "Happiness comes from letting go."

When there is hope for a sequential outcome—finish treatment, finish high school, finish college, successfully enter adulthood—there is also a lot of expectation and pressure. Regardless of whether these expectations are silent or expressed, kids still feel this pressure. When parents have high hopes for change or outcomes, kids will always feel that there is something wrong with who they are today, that they are broken and need to be fixed. In turn, many kids react to this pressure in passive or unconscious ways to oppose their parents' lack of acceptance. Unfortunately, this can also mean more self-destructive behaviors.

I know this is confusing and tricky territory, but the goal is to disrupt stuck patterns in the parent-child relationship. Parents can send their children to treatment so that they learn more-effective ways to manage their thoughts, emotions, or life—but these are skills that parents can also learn. Part of this is accepting the pain and loss associated with their child's struggle.

Still, acceptance brings up a challenging presumption. Many parents feel that being a "good" parent simply means working harder. Parents associate giving up with not caring or even accepting failure. However, this idea is slightly different—when parents really let go, something new can emerge. There can still be hopes and dreams for the future; parents just need to allow themselves to open up to the present unknown.

We have all heard the stories of couples who struggle to conceive, who try fertility treatments and perhaps even begin the paperwork for adoption, who hit their give-up point—only to find themselves pregnant. Giving up does not mean that you don't still want a child—it simply means you are accepting what is. You are stepping away from magical thinking, denial, and distortions, and you are moving toward being rooted in reality.

A parent that I worked with recently asked about hope: "Aren't we supposed to instill a sense of hope in our child?" Well, it's actually not so simple. So often parents state a lot of hopeful or encouraging things when they press their autopilot button:

"It will work out."

"Don't worry."

"You love school, remember?"

"You'll be finished soon; it will be okay."

"It's not that bad."

"Look on the bright side."

These statements begin to sound like the invalidating preprogrammed messages discussed in the previous chapter. The child is feeling sad, frustrated, and upset, and instead of listening and validating the authenticity of the child's experience, parents are trying to fill it with hope. This is a losing battle; we all know how kids can pop holes in our hope balloons. And right underneath hope is fear. Kids need to feel hope from within; we cannot hand it to them from the outside. A child will only move to hope when he or she is ready. In fact, forcing hope can frequently backfire. When a child does not feel heard, frequently he will just spiral into blame by directing his unease back onto the parents, with statements such as "It *is* terrible, and it's your fault." Quickly this attempt of hope-giving can cause a collapse into another argument or a division in the parent-child relationship.

When parents hold on to hope, they are missing where their child is today. Instead, parents can engage in their own growth process. This is change they *can* control. We don't know what the future will hold for our kids, or for anybody for that matter, but parents can know that they are doing their own part. Move away from planning, and move toward the uncertainty of the present moment. This can provide relief.

Paradoxical Approaches

For many of us, accepting pain, confusion, chaos, disappointment, or fear is entirely paradoxical. Many think we are supposed to be fighting back at life. In some cases this may be true, like when you stand up for what you believe in. However, with our own feelings, we do more damage when we fight them. Imagine for a minute any feeling or emotional struggle you have right now. First, oppose it with all your might—then allow yourself to fully feel it and accept it. Most likely the latter brings more relief.

Still, you may be one of those parents who think, "My child will still be mad, sad, anxious, or hopeless, even if I do all the proper listening, reflecting, and validating." Remember that our children *can* still be mad; our job is simply to let them feel. But it's still always good to have a couple more tools in the belt if kids are avoiding life. The paradoxical approach is one of those tools.

Research has shown that paradoxical approaches—especially related to anxiety—are quite effective at reducing symptoms. For example, if someone has a fear of heights, you can say to that person, "It is completely okay to be afraid of heights," rather tell them to just get over it, which actually feeds the stress. When someone says, "Why are you so scared of heights?" the message may be heard as "What is wrong with you?" When someone validates or reassures the anxiety, it actually reduces tension and allows the anxious person to exhale a bit and even begin to relax. A paradoxical approach takes a step closer to the anxiety rather than away. Try saying, "Your anxiety is actually important information from your body. What do you think it's telling you?"

For instance, if a child experiences school anxiety, his dad could tell him, "It is totally okay and normal to feel anxious at school. You can try to fight it, but I think it will still be there. It's better to accept that feeling. What if you let yourself be anxious, or even welcome it? Every day you go to school you are expanding your world—if you are anxious, it means you are growing and expanding. Feeling anxious can be good." Although it's paradoxical and may not make obvious sense, it actually works.

When her daughter is really sad and won't get out of bed, a mother can say, "Your situation sounds really upsetting. I can understand why you feel sad. Perhaps you shouldn't get out of bed until you are ready." This completely flips the situation on its head and also removes any power struggle in the parent-child relationship; it eliminates any gratification that a child may get from defiance. The daughter in this example will get out of bed more quickly because she is not gaining anything from staying in bed, except more sadness. Moreover, when she is heard and validated by her mother, she will process the emotion and feel the impulse to move on. The parent does not oppose the child's emotion and the child does not oppose her own emotion, so the river flows.

Paradoxical approaches are good to experiment with—they essentially take the idea of accepting feelings one step further by framing the negative emotion as a positive. The negative emotion becomes something to accept and discover rather than to fight with a drug, a quart of ice cream, or a video game. Paradoxical approaches continue to send the message that feelings are okay.

Restoring Equilibrium

We all have our own emotional currents. We may not be in charge of what we feel, but I believe we are in charge of how we react and behave in response to those feelings. The same is true for our children—we certainly can't change their feelings, but we can teach them to abide with, accept, and validate what they feel.

With small children, most of us try to direct, manage, and control our children's emotions, by damming up or redirecting their currents. This requires a lot of work and it only works temporarily; it is not sustainable over the long term. Water is pretty powerful, and though with small children it seems we can set up culverts and drains to cheer them up and fix their disappointments, with time the current can become much stronger than we are. Clinical psychologist Wendy Mogel writes in *Blessings of a Skinned Knee* that many children in her practice are repeatedly told how "special" they are, which disrupts many children's equilibrium. She writes: "If the pressure to be special gets too intense, children end up in the therapist's office suffering from sleep and eating disorders, chronic stomachaches, hair-pulling, depression, and other ailments."

What would happen if we just let their rivers run, if we let them feel and be who they are without labels of "good," "bad," "special," or "smart"? When we validate and listen, we accept kids for who they are. *Behaviors* are what we can redirect, not their temperaments or currents of emotions.

Responding to Noah

Noah's family was effectively hooked on hope (of greatness) and fear (of failure). The parents were also damming their own rivers by trying to control their anxiety about their son's future and trying to control and fix him. When Noah dammed his river in response to his feelings of anxiety, he began to experience medical problems; he began to shut down emotionally, avoided life, and even began a computer addiction.

Noah's family can restore equilibrium by allowing themselves to feel their own emotions and accept their life situations. Instead of hovering and tiptoeing around Noah's anxiety to try to keep him on track, his mothers can really let go of managing his feelings and simply hold him accountable for his behavior. Here is an example:

"Noah, we see how anxious you are. I know because I have anxiety myself. I imagine that it's really uncomfortable. I also imagine that ordering your room or playing computer games does provide temporary relief. But we also know that computer games are unhealthy if played to excess. We're going to set a limit of only two hours of computer time each night, which you need to use for your homework. I'm also going to ask that we explore coping skills and techniques that help with anxiety. We can take you to a cognitive-behavioral therapist, a meditation or relaxation class, or perhaps another idea you may have, but we are going to ask that you choose some treatment for your anxiety. We're also going to work on our anxiety as parents; I know that we have worried a lot about you and tried to solve your problems. We want you to solve your own problems, but we're here to help you. We are always here to talk."

Noah's parents can trust that his own natural intelligence and talents will flourish when he learns to better manage his anxiety; they can also listen to and validate Noah's feelings and worries without trying to change them.

Though parents can't direct a child's emotions, they can direct their child's behavior. Parents can set limits with consequences on computer use, disrespect, self-isolating in rooms, and avoiding family life—even for a child with an anxiety disorder—because all these behaviors do is add layers to the problem. Parents can help kids get treatment and encourage the use of effective coping strategies. If Noah makes poor choices, he will face corresponding consequences from both his parents and from his school. There is no need for his parents to manage or interfere with this.

I believe most kids won't change their behavior unless their parents accept, normalize, and validate who they are and what they feel. Having straight As is not as important for a child as being able to build moccasins, as being able to direct his or her own life. When kids feel in charge of themselves, they will be able to utilize their intelligence and gifts.

The Future

Parents can employ these practices and achieve new outcomes in the family; I have seen so many lives transformed this way. When parents become honest and present with their own feelings, they are able to honor and validate their children's feelings. This is, of course, a long-term optimism; I imagine most families will have many ups and downs in the short term, which is why it's important for parents to loosen their grip on planning and scheduling their child's progression. In one, two, or five years there will be considerable movement and an opportunity for a child to grow up, resume his or her emotional development, and successfully integrate the gains of these parenting practices. If parents attach hope and fear to every therapist report, every report card, every evaluation, there will be an increase in suffering. Yet with time and trust, parents can stay steady, stay with their feelings, and refrain from overinvolvement, and kids will build their moccasins.

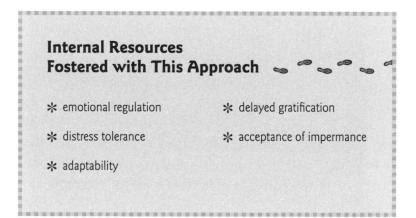

Internal Resources Fostered with This Approach

* emotional regulation

* distress tolerance

* adaptability

* delayed gratification

* acceptance of impermance

CHAPTER 3

Skill: Letting Your Child's River Run

The key to listening to another's dreams is to keep that person working
and processing, rather than putting yourself in the position
of needing to have all the answers.
—**Thomas Bien,** *Mindful Therapy*

What do you do when your child feels pain? What is the difference between emotional attunement and emotional rescuing? Do your responses to your child come from a place of compassion or fear? These are critical questions—if your underlying motives are to rescue your children from struggle because you are afraid of them feeling pain, chances are you are laying down the leather and damming the currents of their feelings. (And most likely your own as well.)

When we let their rivers run, we let our children experience their full range of feelings, which is a normal part of the human experience. We should set limits on or simply ignore (rather than gratifying with attention) inappropriate behaviors—excessive whining, yelling, inappropriate expression of anger, bullying, self-identifying as a victim, emotional manipulation, shutting down and isolating, and defiance—but we shouldn't try to change their emotions. Kids are allowed to have a bad day. We must ask ourselves why our kids' happiness is our "job."

Much of the seemingly empathy-based parenting that has taken root in our culture today is really fear-based when you scratch just beneath the surface. What are we so afraid of?

Fear-Based Parenting

Let's call it what it is. When parents walk on eggshells in their own home to accommodate their child's moods and sensitivities, worried about doing something wrong and upsetting their child—this behavior is driven by fear. When parents sleep with their children night after night, even when they want to stop and doing so is interfering with their lives, marriages, and careers—fear again is the undercurrent of the home. Fear that their child is too fragile to sleep alone, fear that their child may get angry or feel sad. When parents find themselves making all sorts of excuses for their child's poor behavior, overlooking disrespect, and even tolerating verbal or emotional abuse from their child, they are motivated by fear. When parents edit and supervise every homework assignment up until and even into their child's college years, this is fear-based parenting. No wonder our kids are anxious.

Unfortunately, many parents feel that these extreme measures are a sign of dedication to their child. But we must ask ourselves whether we're dedicated to teaching our children to build their own moccasins or whether we're dedicated to a life of laying down leather. Both kinds of parents—moccasin builders and leather layers—love their children; the issue is not love, the issue is fear. Hovering parents are afraid of their child experiencing pain—because they themselves are afraid of feeling pain.

Unfortunately, we're not helping our kids by bending over backward to accommodate them; this makes them dependent on us. We need to teach them to be independent by incrementally handing over the reins.

If we say that parents are 100 percent responsible for the well-being of an infant and perhaps hope to be 0 percent responsible for a twenty-five-year-old, parents have to incrementally hand responsibility over to their kids. So, if we use this logic, parents should be responsible for around 50 percent of the well-being of their twelve-and-a-half-year-old. What that means is half of the preteen's care rests in her own lap. This includes waking up on her own; dressing herself; washing herself; preparing her breakfast and packing her lunch; organizing her room and school backpack; contributing to household chores such as cooking, laundry, or walking the dog; being responsible for completing her homework; being accountable to her family through working on unhealthy behaviors; following through on household rules and expectations; going to sleep at bedtime;

and so on. Parents still do the shopping and most of the cooking and cleaning, drive their children to their school/activities, pay the bills, and hold their kids accountable when they are acting out, but parents should not encroach into their child's territory.

Today, however, most teens and preteens who have parents in the professional middle class are hovered over by parents who still take 75–90 percent of the responsibility for their child's well-being and education. If the child has any special needs or mental health struggles, that number tends to jump to 90–99 percent. With this dynamic, kids frequently display passivity and traits of helplessness, while parents have surrendered their lives and personalities to parenting. Kids need to be invested in their own lives, their own futures, and the outcomes of their own decisions. This is quite possible even for a child with a learning disability, emotional sensitivity, or mental health disorder.

How do parents step away from fear-based parenting? By slowly removing the dams, all the extra work behind the scenes, and simply letting their children have their own feelings. This may mean the child is mad at the parent for a while, because the parent is not doing as much for the child anymore. That is okay; we need to let children be in charge of their own feelings—and their own lives.

Listening Skills

The next time your child comes to you or calls you on the phone with a negative emotion, rather than trying to fix or cheer up your loved one (or feel frustrated or disappointed that it is your job to do this), you can really let go and listen. On the next page are some examples of emotional attunement—not emotional rescuing—using the steps outlined in chapter 1.

These types of responses will allow you to listen to your child's feelings; in these responses you are allowing the child's currents to flow. You are allowing the child's emotion to stay in his department. You are sending the message that you believe your child is capable of solving his own problem.

As a listener, you're conveying acceptance. Chances are good that your child will move on emotionally after being heard. Kids shift on their own when they're ready. Letting them keep their feelings celebrates the textures of life.

1) Focus on the child's emotion rather than the content of the problem (school, friends, dinner, homework, etc.). For example, if the child says any of the following, what is he or she really feeling?

"I can't do anything right"

"You make me so mad."

"That is so unfair."

"Whatever."

"You don't care about me."

"It is all Billy's fault."

2) Reflect the feelings back to your child.

"You sound upset."

"I see that you're angry."

"You look exhausted, sweetie."

"You sound really frustrated."

"You sound sad."

3) Become curious.

"What happened?"

"Did something happen between you and Jenna?"

"Can you tell me more about it?"

"You know, your sadness sounds important; what do you think is there?"

"I can see that you went to your room, but I don't know what you're thinking or feeling; do you want to talk about it?"

"I can try to imagine why you may be in bed but I don't really know. Can you tell me what you're feeling?"

4) When your child responds, validate his or her feelings.

"That is anxiety provoking!"

"How disappointing!"

"That's frustrating."

"That sounds hard."

"That is difficult."

"It is scary to do that."

5) Let your child be in charge of solving the problem.
   "What do you think you'll do?"
   "How do you think you'll cope with it?"
   "Is there a way for you to problem-solve?"
   "What will you do about it?"

6) Stay away from fixing and solving at all costs, and only offer your advice if your child specifically asks.
   "I am here if you want to talk more."
   "You're good at solving stuff like this."
   "You got this."

I-Feel Statements

Taking a long walk, meditation, journaling—these are some of the many ways adults can tune in to their own feelings. Becoming aware of your feelings is not some New Agey suggestion; it is essential for moccasin building. Parents can become more self-aware through developing self-reflective practices. Frequently when parents are reacting to situations, behaviors, or events, they are frantically searching for solutions outside of themselves and reaching for quick fixes, instead of consulting with their own truths or intuitions.

Parents need to become clear about what they feel. In enmeshed parent-child relationships it can be quite blurry who is feeling what, because parents are busy taking care of their child's emotions—anticipating what their child may be feeling, assuming their child is mad or upset, and following a course of behaviors based on that assumption. Parents are only responsible for their own feelings and behaviors, and likewise, kids are only responsible for their feelings and behaviors. Parents can't have real dialogue and be emotionally attuned with their children if they don't know their own emotions.

A critical way to differentiate what a parent is feeling and what a child is feeling is the use of I-feel statements. I-feel statements communicate to children that parents are three-dimensional human beings—with their own thoughts and feelings. When children are disrespectful or lie, parents have their own thoughts and feelings related to this behavior. Parents might feel sad, worried, angry, or powerless—and kids need to know how they impact others.

When parents let go of managing their children and realize that their job is just to manage their own thoughts and feelings, this can free parents up to be assertive and clear. When parents become clear in their emotional awareness, thinking, and communication, they will be much clearer in their parenting. A metaphor I frequently use with my clients is that parents need to "clean up their side of the street." When parents get their emotional houses in order, clean up their own messes, and communicate in a way that is clear and centered, then parents are reclaiming their power.

Just as we cannot tell a child her feeling is right or wrong, the same applies to us. When a child is sad, scared, ashamed, or upset, that is simply her experience. When parents are clear and aware of their own feelings, there is no right or wrong; there's simply the parent's experience. It's important for parents to identify feeling words: *angry, sad, worried,* and *overwhelmed*. When parents have a clear awareness about what they feel, parents will have a clearer sense of how to communicate and respond.

The I-feel statement is the most effective tool I have come across for clear communication. It's even useful for inner dialogue; putting our thoughts and emotions into this format requires us to slow down and fine tune our inner landscape. This format allows us to be assertive and accountable for what we feel. Most importantly, I-feel statements take away the "you." When we take away the "you-statement," we are stepping away from blame and toward real dialogue. It goes as follows:

I feel _____ (emotion)
I feel this way when _____ (event)
I feel this because I think _____ (thought, belief)
My hope / plan / question is _____ (action)

When parents clean up their side of the street and step away from blame, it exposes the child's messy yard; parents are modeling accountability. They are stepping away from power struggles and toward clear dialogue, and fostering parent-child differentiation. We have to stop managing our children's messes; children will only clean up their messes when they realize no one else will, when they realize it's their responsibility, it's their life. Cleaning up our own messes is actually quite empowering.

A Straightforward Example

I feel sad.

I feel this way when you use a disrespectful tone in your voice with me.

I feel this way because I believe that we need to communicate with respect with people we love.

My hope is that you can tell me what you are feeling, rather than use an aggressive tone. I hope you will let me know if I use a disrespectful tone with you.

An Informal Example

I feel concerned when I see you bully your brother. I wonder what you are feeling that may cause you to act this way. Can you tell me what you are feeling?

An Interactive Example

Mother: I feel upset and sad to hear that you lied about where you went after school. Can you tell me what happened?

Daughter: Well, I was going to call you, but Jinny changed the plan and she gave me some candy and asked me to promise not to call you.

Mother: How did you feel about that?

Daughter: I didn't like it.

Mother: What can you do differently next time?

Daughter: I don't know. She always has candy, and she made me promise.

Mother: Sweetie, you are only responsible for you and your choices. She may do this every day—is there something else that you can do?

Daughter: Well, I can tell her that she is not in charge of me.

Mother: Okay, that sounds good. Just so you know, in life, you will be the one who receives the consequence for lying, not Jinny.

Daughter: I know.

An I-Feel Statement with a Boundary

I feel powerless and confused.

I feel this way when you stay in bed and refuse school and show disrespect toward me and then get out of bed to see your friends.

I feel this way because I do not know what to do when you shut down.

I can't control if you go to school, but I cannot allow you to call or see friends that day. We will not make it so easy for you to pick not going to school and still choose to see your friends. Seeing friends means engaging in a full life, which includes school.

Asking Children What They Feel—Allowing a Gap

When we ask children what they feel, we are asking them to be self-aware, to engage, to share, and to participate in the family. Of course we don't know if they will share, which creates a gap of uncertainty. But when parents "rescue" a child's perceived discomfort, these efforts are to control uncertainty, and they are meddling in the child's domain and fostering dependency, not participation.

If your child goes to his room, slams the door, and refuses to talk to you, there could be a myriad of reasons your child has chosen this behavior. Many parents go to work right away to try to figure it out, and make all sorts of assumptions about what is happening, which I call "filling in the gaps." For example, a parent might assume the child is mad at the parent, or the parent might assume the child was bullied that day. When a parent does not really know what a child is thinking or feeling, yet follows a course of action based on an assumption, this is a parent's effort to fill in any uncertainty. When parents fill in the gaps, they are not asking the child to be accountable for his part in the parent-child relationship. Instead, parents can stop and go to the child and ask what he is thinking and feeling—this increases a parent's ability to understand a child's inner world.

In emotional attunement, parents simply mirror the observable facts;

they don't work tirelessly behind the scenes to fill in the gaps. So a parent might say, "I see that you are upset, I see that you slammed your door, I see that you have chosen to stay in your room. But these behaviors do not tell me what you are thinking or feeling. I am here to listen if you want to talk about it." Then the parent leaves it on the child's lap. The parent is allowing a gap to be there—which can be scary. Typically, parents are good at jumping to conclusions and thinking that they know what is going on. Frequently this angers the child more.

In this scenario, the parent is not encroaching into the child's territory. Rather, the parent is respecting the child's boundary, yet the parent is also opening the door to dialogue by attuning and saying, "I see you and I am here." In this sense the parent is going toward feelings and away from fixing.

Eventually the son responds to his parent and opens his bedroom door:

Son, responding to his parent's inquiry by using an I-feel statement: "I'm just angry that Connor was really mean today."

Parent, expressing empathy, validation, and curiosity: "Oh, that sounds difficult, did something happen?"

Son: "Well, he won't let me play with their group at recess."

Parent, validating and encouraging problem solving: "That sounds painful; kids can be really mean. What do you think you will do?"

Son: "Well, Jeff and Brian always play soccer at recess, so I guess I can play with them."

Parent, being curious: "Do you like them?"

Son: "Yeah, they're good friends."

Parent: "Well, sounds like a good choice. Thanks for telling me how you feel. Is there anything more?"

Son: "I just have a big project to do tonight."

Parent: "Okay, well let me know if you need help."

When parents attune without fixing, this often leads to sharing feelings. When parents refrain from filling in the gaps of what their kids think and feel, children actually step forward and do it themselves.

In many of my workshops I have noticed that parents are very uncomfortable with this gap. They constantly want to build a bridge to the child's domain, so the child does not feel so alone, sad, angry, worried. They think leaving a gap is some sort of abandonment. Although it can be scary to try something new in the parent-child relationship, this gap allows a space for something new to emerge: a vulnerable space.

I'll share an example. My older daughter had to leave a special end-of-the-year party because her younger sister was sick. In the ride home, my older daughter, still eight, sounded like a teenager on a rampage, blasting into my husband all the reasons he is ruining her life. My husband cycled through all the thoughts in his head. He first wanted to fix her feeling by turning around and driving back, even though our younger daughter was passed out in the car. He then wanted to yell back, to get her to stop, because her yelling was triggering his anger. Then he wanted to negotiate with her about what we would get her instead, if she quieted down. Finally he ultimately did what we practice, which is to validate. He said, "I hear how sad and frustrated and angry you feel." When my husband did not engage he allowed all the emotion to stay on my daughter's lap. This left a gap. He did not make it better—sometimes kids get sick and plans change. However the next morning, my daughter made a point of bridging the gap herself; she came to my husband and apologized for how poorly she treated him and said how sorry she was for her behavior, and she apologized to her sister.

In my experiences gaps are frequently filled with children stepping forward and sharing more, which creates a richer parent-child relationship. This may not happen overnight, and it requires parents to stay with uncertainty, but it can shift the dynamic; instead of the parent pursuing the child and the child distancing, both can equally share and engage in the relationship.

This is intimacy and closeness in the parent-child relationship. Parents have a choice: Do I want to relate to my kids through fixing or through sharing? Emotional attunement and I-feel statements are a critical way for kids to process and regulate emotions, and tolerate distress—all key ingredients for moccasins.

Assignment: Free Writing for Your Journal

1) What do you need to do to more deeply accept your child and his or her struggles?

2) What is preventing you from accepting your present feelings/ situation?

3) What happens if you touch into the pain and fear underneath your behavior?

4) Can you step away from hope and fear and accept where your child is today?

5) Can you communicate in an I-feel statement?

PART II

Nature:
The Cause and Effect of Behaviors

CHAPTER 4

Holding Up a Mirror to Our Children's Behavior

··

When we fall on the ground it hurts us,
but we also need to rely on the ground in order to get back up.
—**Kathleen McDonald,** *How to Meditate*

··

A hallmark of leather laying is when parents' efforts are aimed at "getting through the day," rather than giving children the necessary limits and boundaries to struggle with, to build skills for the future. Because I largely work with parents of teens, many of these children are now eighteen, and yet they are still emotionally much younger than their ages, because their parents worked so hard to get them through the semester, school year, winter break, summer, and so on. Parents are doing all the "efforting," which removes responsibility and the maturation process from kids.

Why are parents doing so much efforting? One of the reservations we have concerning setting and enforcing limits for our children is that we may upset them. Many parents think that a large part of their job is to comfort feelings and cheer their kids up, so parents wrestle with thoughts like "How do I give a consequence for my child's poor behavior when he may cry and feel angry—aren't I *also* suppose to soothe him?" Many parents flip-flop back and forth between setting limits and then removing them and comforting their child. This ambiguity actually disrupts the moccasin-building process, because kids are rescued from their feelings and from facing consequences. Consequences, however—whether natural or logical—provide a mirror, which is a parent's best friend.

In many of his books and lectures the Dalai Lama speaks of self-discipline. He says that all discipline *is* self-discipline. If discipline comes from the outside, it is hegemony. Of course children are not born with self-discipline—it is learned. The Dalai Lama elaborates in *Advice on Dying* that self-discipline only comes when we are aware of or experience consequences. Consequences are really gifts that steer and guide behavior. As an example, he shares a story of having stomach flu. Despite liking spicy and sour foods, while sick, he had to refrain from these to care for his stomach. In this sense he was disciplined. This type of natural consequence gave him feedback in the moment about his food choices. Tibetan Buddhist teacher Chogyam Trungpa Rinpoche says in *Smile at Fear* that the world is always giving us feedback; any choice we make, positive or negative, has corresponding feedback about actions we make or actions we avoid. We can trust that there will always be a response from the world.

If we don't do our homework, we may fail the class. If we don't go to work one day, we may lose our job. If we treat our spouse/partner poorly, he or she may choose to end the relationship. We all have choices every day, and natural consequences inform our choices. There is always cause and effect; there is always a mirror. The same exists for positive choices: if I work hard at my job, I may advance my career; if I work hard at school, I may learn and get good grades; if I treat my spouse well, I may have a happy marriage. Of course, good choices do not always equal happiness, as life is unpredictable, but awareness of positive and negative consequences certainly does help us more successfully navigate life.

This response from the world—this cause and effect—can be relied upon by parents, as it means we don't have to intervene and direct; we can allow the natural course of things to happen. For example, if your child forgets his snack, he will be hungry; if your child forgets his hat and mittens, he will be cold; if your child kicks a hole in his bedroom wall, it will be there to remind him of his anger. None of these consequences are safety issues, so we don't need to layer on more negatives or try to fix the problem. Yet how many parents work hard to remove consequences and also remain frustrated that their children are not responsible?

We all have the capacity to self-regulate based on the natural consequences of our choices. In the adult world, natural consequences seem to be lurking around every corner. If you forget to feed your meter, you get a parking ticket; if you send your bills in late, you accrue a late fee;

if you don't buy enough food, there may be nothing to eat for dinner—there are constant reminders of consequences for adults. Yet for kids, skipping a chore, yelling at a parent, playing endless video games, or avoiding homework might not invoke an obvious natural consequence. Still, I believe these behaviors elicit natural consequences in subtle ways: a child's self-esteem may drop when he mistreats his parents, a child will not feel a sense of contributing to the family if he shirks his chores, and his education is impacted by avoiding homework, for instance.

But since these subtle natural consequences are implied rather than explicit, parents have to also hold up a mirror and create an additional *logical* consequence for their child. I recently heard a story on the radio about a weight-loss program that a corporation was offering to its employees as part of their health plan. A group that chose to participate committed to attending one of the many exercise classes that the corporation offered each day. Each week the group met for support and to assess how well they were achieving their goals. The group all agreed that they needed a consequence to keep them on track, so they came up with a logical one. They devised a sign-in system for each class—if a member of the group missed an exercise class, that person had to come to their next meeting in his or her bathing suit. As you can imagine no one missed an exercise class, and their group was deemed successful.

Awareness of consequences tend to keep us on task. For children to develop self-discipline, children must experience both the natural and the logical consequences of their choices—perhaps not humiliation, but a loss of a privilege. Kids have to have some investment—some skin in the game—that their behavior is real, with real consequences. Some good examples might be leaving a party early for pushing another kid, losing a night out after breaking curfew, losing computer privileges for looking at inappropriate content, or simply losing a mother's attention after showing disrespect. We can still be compassionate to their feelings, but we cannot take away consequences because then our kids will never learn this precious skill of self-regulation. We are not doing kids any favors by skipping or removing consequences. These mirrors we hold up as parents allow children to see what they are doing, to experience a consequence, and to adjust their behavior—this helps them build their moccasins.

Many parents feel it's "mean" to give a logical consequence, because children are upset when they lose a privilege. Furthermore, many parents meddle in an attempt to remove other natural consequences in a child's life: asking a teacher to change a poor grade, talking to a coach to get a child more field time, paying a child's excessive cell phone bill, or hiring an expensive lawyer when a child gets in trouble with the law. Parents work hard to mitigate their children's struggles. All of these responses can be understandable, but if we see life as a journey on a rocky trail, removing one bump does not help a kid prepare for the bigger boulder that's around the bend. Before kids have the chance to get in trouble with the law, it is best that they struggle safely in the home with made-up consequences.

Gratitude for Small Struggles

Small, contained struggles are good. Though unpleasant for parents, struggles around homework, cleaning a room, or following through with tasks are precisely where we want kids to learn how to build their moccasins. This is the fertile soil for skill-development. I would much rather have my daughters struggle daily in the home and learn to master tasks, chores, homework, and respectful communication than for them to have a more adult struggle outside the home without having the tools to deal with it. Parents can reframe all these small struggles—to see them positively and even be grateful to them. For example, having your child experience rejection or failure in the fourth grade can be a great blessing. Yet many parents today go on attack when their child has any negative experience at school.

When parents see that the home is the rich soil where endless daily lessons regarding choices, behavior, consequences, and staying with discomfort are learned, there does not need to be a negative tone attached to children's behavior. When parents ask an older sibling to take a break after shoving a younger sibling, there does not need to be a tone of "I am so disappointed with you!" When we shame or blame our children they simply build up a wall and most likely miss the lesson of the consequence. If we say instead, "I feel sad when you use a threatening tone in your voice" or "I feel concerned when I see you pushing your brother," we can communicate in ways that continue to give kids information about how they impact others. Parents can then provide the logical consequence.

This feedback, communicated through I-feel statements and logical consequences, is directed at modifying the child's behavior—rather than at labeling the child as "good" or "bad." Parents have to distinguish the person from the behavior. Kids can always adjust their behavior from looking in the mirror or experiencing a consequence. Remember, consequences and struggle are good; this is the process of moccasin building.

Jillian

Though Jillian had just turned fifteen, her maturity level more closely resembled a twelve-year-old. She was pretty and popular yet extremely inhibited in all areas of her life, except her clothing choices. She had the ability to pull off any outfit or look, and since she knew the right way to push her parent's buttons, she was able to get new clothes whenever she wanted. Yet, upon closer inspection, Jillian knew how to do little by herself.

She has twin younger brothers, and growing up her mother always felt terrible about how abruptly she had to adjust to two new babies in the home. Jillian had been an only child for three and a half years, and she had a close bond with her mom. When the twins came, her mother worked hard to not alter her life too much and to still have a lot of alone time with her. As you can imagine, Jillian's mother, Donna, was stretched thin. Donna's husband was a successful professional so the family had resources; when Donna was unable to fill the gap in Jillian's life with her attention, she filled it with gifts.

Any time there was an upset in Jillian's life, Donna worked hard to cheer up, fix, or rescue her from struggle. In fact this became their bond, their script, the template in their parent-child relationship. Jillian never had to be accountable for her own struggles and emotions, because these fell into her mother's jurisdiction. Not surprisingly, Jillian would turn on her mother and even get mad at her when anything was askew. This included frequent disrespect, snapping, eye-rolling, blaming, and at times harsh criticisms of her mother—yet this only caused her mother to work harder and harder to hover and fix.

Jillian adored her brothers about 20 percent of the time, but mostly she was annoyed with them and cold in response to them. She would blame them for her feelings of sadness and frustration, which created constant tension in the home. Yet Donna continued to toil away in an attempt to keep the peace. In response to Jillian's moods, Donna asked little of Jillian around the home and even hired a tutor to sit with her nightly to help with her homework—Donna was worried about college and wanted Jillian to develop good study habits.

By the eighth grade, Jillian had few areas of strength to rely on. She had always played soccer, but half-heartedly; it seemed more of a social outlet than a real interest. She was able to maintain Bs, but she mostly enjoyed reading text messages not books. She lacked drive in almost all areas in her life. Her parents still ordered her meals when they went out to eat, organized her schedule, cleaned her room, and in all ways worked hard to make life smooth in the home. Yet they frequently had an irritable, moody young lady on their hands.

When Jillian hit ninth grade, she walled off her parents even more. She only went to them when she wanted something, so they treasured this small connection that they had with her—resulting in too many material indulgences. Jillian began to dress in increasingly mature ways and began to get the attention of older boys. She eventually started dating a junior named Will, which she kept a secret. Her parents continued to worry about college and grades, so they gave her more rein in her social life, as long as she did her homework. Meanwhile, Will was not very nice to Jillian and would alternate between treating her poorly and treating her like a princess.

As Jillian was still quite young emotionally, she had enough inhibition to avoid intercourse, yet she was willing to try other things with Will. He got her to pose for racy pictures and introduced her to oral sex. Though uncomfortable with her sexuality, Jillian got a high from taking risks. She lacked esteem boosts through school or extracurriculars, so Will's validation and attention was addictive. Moreover, Jillian liked having secrets from her mother, feeling that she had something that was her own, since her mother hovered over everything else. Her newfound independence felt intoxicating.

However, when he came up against her unwillingness to have intercourse, Will eventually moved on for a girl his own age. Jillian had no skills to deal with this rejection and sank into a deep depression. She had always relied on her mother to cushion her and manage her emotions, but she did not know how to tell her mother about this. She refused to get out of bed for a week and even entertained suicidal thoughts.

Eventually Jillian made her way into my office. When asking her parents about patterns and dynamics in the family system, Donna reported that Jillian was their guinea pig, being their first child, so they never knew the "right" age to ask her to do things for herself. They knew homework was important but thought their job as parents was to help their daughter and fix her struggles. When asked about rules and boundaries, Donna revealed that rules were constantly in flux, depending on each situation. What became apparent was that Jillian had no self-management skills and was not only emotionally immature but was also deeply dependent on her mother, emotionally and otherwise.

Without moccasins she had badly cut up her feet. As she was exposed to more mature struggles outside the home—boyfriends and sexuality Jillian had no ability to cope, as she had not developed skills or tools inside the home.

Parenting without Limits

Through years of working as an adolescent therapist and parent coach, I have inquired into whether limits and boundaries existed in my clients' family systems. Although most families professed that they *did* have rules, I was more interested in whether a "no" meant "no" or whether a "no" meant "no, maybe." I should note that I scarcely saw a child in therapy who had healthy parental limits and boundaries to struggle within.

My subjective results over the years broke down into four groups: (1) parents who made up rules and limits on a moment-to-moment basis, which were easily negotiated by the child; (2) parents who found limits futile because their kids acted unaffected by consequences—for example, they wanted to be in their room and didn't care if they could not go out; (3) parents who gave up on rules because their kids were so defiant;

(4) parents who were simply so needy and emotionally dependent on their kids for a relationship that they dropped all rules. Of course, on occasion I met with a child in a rare, fifth category: one with strong executive functioning skills who was overcompetent in the organization and self-care category. I found that these were high-functioning kids from more neglectful homes; they'd found that if they wanted to get something done, they had to make it happen themselves. Anecdotally I would say 90–95 percent of the kids I saw in treatment programs had parents with poor boundaries, meaning they did not have set rules or hold their children accountable.

Professor Margaret Nelson has directed quite a bit of attention to this area in her book *Parenting Out of Control.* She cites that through her research two distinct groups formed: parents with limits and parents without limits. Interestingly, these limits correspond to education and class differences. She groups parents not merely on income but also social class, which has material, educational, and cultural elements. The parents deemed the "professional middle class" have largely adopted this style of "parenting out of control." She writes:

> Professional middle-class parents want both to protect their children from growing up too quickly and to push them to high achievement at an early age. The latter impulse often leads to treating children as peers and to claiming that those children can be trusted to make decisions on their own; the former impulse often leads to hovering.

Working and middle-class (nonprofessional) parents fall into the "parenting with limits" category. Nelson notes that these parents "are more concerned with skills that will ensure self-sufficiency than they are with passion and fun." Some of the limits imposed by the parents in this category are purely financial; others relate to parents who perhaps face many limits in their own lives.

Professional middle- and upper-class parents sense there are fewer limits in life—hence fewer limits in parenting. This is not based on their income level alone, as the income of professional parents varies greatly, but instead on their education, which perhaps taught them anything is possible. Although the sense of possibility is a wonderful thing, it can lead to skipping over limits and rules and avoiding struggles with their kids. This removes the cause from effect and interferes with a young person's development of internal organization and resources.

It should also be noted that the majority of the professional middle-class parents employ markedly different parenting practices than their parents, who set clear limits. The pendulum has swung from the more authoritarian parenting of the previous generation to the current "child-centered" parenting, moving the trend to the nontraditional parenting practices of today. The hallmarks of this trend are an overfocus on children's happiness (as opposed to emotional health), emotional and material indulgences, school and activity-oriented success to help boost their esteem, and negotiable rules and parental hovering, resulting in less independent and less resilient children.

Interestingly, the way many professional middle-class parents find control is not through clear limits with consequences but through surveillance. *Surveillance* means not only closely supervising the child within the home but also monitoring them through technology—via texts, cell phones, Facebook, GPS tracking through the child's phone—and even spying on them. These parents eschew boundaries and rules in an attempt to gain connection and closeness with their kids, and then try to control their children through hovering.

Professor Barbara Hofer calls this "the electronic tether." What started out as a curiosity—more and more kids walking around Middlebury College with cell phones glued to their ears, talking to their parents—became interesting research indicating sharp changes in parental involvement in their child's college life. A thorough survey of the entire student body at Middlebury and another institution revealed that the average number of times parents and children communicated (whether through phone, text, email, etc.) was 13.4 times per week. This research signifies a monumental shift—from the obligatory weekly call previous generations made home from their college dorm room to the electronic tether Hofer describes today. Also evident on college campuses is the corresponding emotional immaturity in eighteen- to twenty-two-year-olds. Hofer writes in *The iConnected Parent*:

Based on our extensive surveys of Middlebury and Michigan students, the bottom line is that *students who have the most frequent contact with their parents are less autonomous than other students.* They are least likely to have achieved some of the psychological benchmarks of independence that in the past would have been typical of this age, according to standard psychological tests included in the surveys.

Whether a child struggles with mental health in high school or seems to continue on a more "normal" path to college, if parents are overinvolved and hovering, this still interferes with their child's individuation and maturation process. This "closeness" comes at the child's expense.

The Tables Have Turned

Starting out in the field of wilderness therapy in my early twenties, I began to observe these overinvolved and delicate parent-child dynamics, which I found both troubling and baffling. Growing up, and even still today, I always wanted to impress or please my parents—though still maintaining my independence, of course. What I frequently observed in treatment settings was actually the reverse: parents who wanted to impress or please their kids. Rather than a child fearing an upset parent, or worrying about breaking a rule, or losing a parent's trust, parents were actually afraid of their kids; they worried about upsetting their children by not doing exactly want they wanted.

I initially thought this must be a small segment of the population; I figured I'd found the reason why the child is in wilderness therapy and why the parents are getting stuck. Yet as I became a parent myself, I saw that these patterns are pervasive across the spectrum, especially in the socioeconomic category I fall into: the professional middle class. I also began to see the mentality shift in the younger generation of wilderness field instructors, some of whom identified strongly with how entitled the kids in the program felt. One instructor said to me, "I blamed my parents for everything; they brought me into the world, and so they should fix my problems."

At some point in parenting the tables turned from children feeling grateful for parents giving them life (with of course some resentments mixed in), to children feeling resentful toward their parents when experiencing any discomfort in life. Kids today hurl their upsets and disappointments right at their parents, and most of the time parents jump to action. I think the question that needs to be asked is "Whose life is it?" Who is responsible for the child's discomfort—the parent or the child?

Merged Boundaries

Enmeshment, or merged parent-child boundaries, as seen with Jillian and Donna, is a phenomena seen today in both treatment and mainstream settings. When kids have a sense of self that is merged with their parents, they don't feel their own successes and their own failures. Failures are cushioned or mitigated, and successes are guided. The resulting lack of autonomy children have weighs heavily on their emerging sense of selves. It may be convenient for kids to blame their parents when they feel angry or sad, but when it is a parent's job to fix these emotions, a sense of powerlessness in the child's life ensues.

An example I frequently give parents is this: If your child is walking down a path and trips, you might feel that you have a responsibility as a parent to pick him up, but this also instills a sense of helplessness in the child, who must wait to be picked up. In this dynamic the child feels that falling is not his fault nor is getting up his responsibility. This child does not feel in control and in charge of his life. It is no surprise that a child in an enmeshed relationship is more likely to experience the depression and anxiety associated with a lack of self-efficacy and autonomy. Yet how many parents hover (literally and metaphorically) over tripped children?

If a child feels responsible for his own life, he may have to work a little harder than he likes to watch out for obstacles while navigating life, but if he does fall he can get up right away. This builds autonomy, self-direction, problem-solving skills, and a sense of independence.

What is missing from limit-less parenting is the child's sense of "I." Limits and boundaries allow kids to feel that their life is their own—this is empowering. When children face positive or negative consequences for their successes or failures they are more likely to be accountable for their own lives. When kids know that a change in their own behavior can produce a new outcome, young people begin to develop self-control and self-direction.

This boundary between parent and child is of course blurry with newborns, infants, and toddlers, yet even one minute after a baby is born she has her own independent experience of the world. Even the most attentive parent, working hard to give the perfect feeding and nap, must realize that we cannot always fix children's feelings. Some babies still cry. When they become old enough, parents can begin to teach kids to be with their own discomforts, normalizing and validating all feelings—even if the discomfort is caused by a parent's actions, such as bringing a new baby into the family, moving to a new state, taking a job out of the home, and so on.

To cultivate autonomy and independence in young people, we must allow them to have their own thoughts and feelings and also experience their own consequences—this breaks the enmeshment.

In today's parenting culture, we have removed the mirror and removed as many consequences as we can from our children's lives. We keep thinking that if we can control as much as possible, they may attain some sort of pain-free, smooth life. Yet, as portrayed by Jillian, lack of struggle never equaled happiness. It is no surprise that today many kids lack self-discipline. And without an ability to set goals and achieve on their own in life, many kids are faced with more dire struggles such as depression, anxiety, helplessness, and despair. Moreover, parenting has become a backbreaking job, as most all items related to children fall into the parent's domain. This is not sustainable for us and it is certainly not helping our kids. I believe we can restore balance again by trusting in the laws of nature and allowing our children to experience consequences.

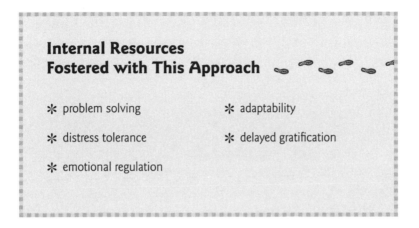

**Internal Resources
Fostered with This Approach**

✳ problem solving   ✳ adaptability

✳ distress tolerance   ✳ delayed gratification

✳ emotional regulation

CHAPTER 5
The Relief of Nature

....

Surrendering does not involve preparing for a soft landing; it means just landing on hard, ordinary ground, on rocky wild countryside. Once we open ourselves, then we land on *what is*.

—**Chogyam Trungpa,** *Cutting through Spiritual Materialism*

....

The natural world imparts a reality that makes the laws of cause and effect clear. If it rains, it's wet outside. If it's windy on a hillside, there is erosion. There are no shortcuts, loopholes, or special treatments in nature. You can't press the "undo" button. If it's cold and kids don't put on a jacket, they will be uncomfortable. If they are thirsty, they have to hike to the creek. If they cut a corner by setting up a flimsy shelter, they may have a rough night. If they stall all morning to get organized, they may have to hike into the night to get to their next campsite. These temporary discomforts inform their choices. Kids have to work with the forces of nature because they can't maneuver around them. This is actually a relief to them.

There is no hovering parent in wilderness programs and so kids have to be resourceful, to problem-solve, to manage time, and to live with the outcome if they don't. They find out that they are capable and they have choices. The immediate feedback offered in nature is refreshing, in our world of quick fixes and convenience. There is little instant gratification—what is valued is the process. Kids have to experience the long hike up a mountain to get the view from the top. A view from a summit is not as appreciated or impactful when a helicopter takes you there—blood and sweat connects us to the real world and to our selves. Limits, boundaries, and consequences are readily available in the wilderness. Kids gain from these limits, even in simple ways. Many kids eat foods such as oats, beans, and lentils that they would normally never eat because there is only one dinner prepared, because all food is carried on their backs. Kids are grateful to eat these foods and to rest by the fire at night. The limits instill character, humility, hard work, creativity, and resourcefulness, and ultimately kids gain internal feelings of happiness. Surprisingly, many defiant, anxious, or disorganized kids love the wilderness. There is a built-in daily structure—the day starts when the sun rises, meal times are regular, there's daily exercise with hikes and games, camp chores happen at dusk before the sun sets, and sitting around an evening fire brings relaxation and natural conversations—which is refreshing. Though at times it's uncomfortable, life feels simple, and kids experience direct contact with the present moment.

To have cause without effect, as is the case in homes without proper limits, disrupts the nature of reality. When kids yell at their parents every day without clear consequences or effect, typically they don't adjust their behavior; they just continue on the next day. Some parents even feed the negative behavior with strong emotional reactions—which are rewards, in a way, because an emotional response from a parent can feel like connection. We don't respond with strong emotion to strangers, only to people we love. Our reactions to our children's tantrums give them lots of attention. Paradoxically when children do something that is expected of them—like going to school—nothing happens. When kids don't do something that is expected—if they refuse to go to school—they tend to receive a lot of parental attention.

When we turn down the volume on our emotional reactions, when we don't provide an audience and instead give children consequences, we provide a sense of personal investment for children in their own choices. If a child chooses not to go to school, parents can simply state a consequence—no TV, computer, or social time, for instance. Instead of gaining attention, the kid is simply losing something that he or she wants. In my experience, when kids don't have mirrors and limits at home, they just push until they find something secure.

How can we ground our parenting in the laws of nature, and in ideas such as cause and effect, so kids know how to adjust their behavior?

Mack

Mack was a tall and skinny thirteen-year-old who knew how to control adults but didn't know how to direct his own self. When he was admitted in the wilderness treatment program he didn't seem to have any particular diagnosis; Mack had perplexed therapists, school counselors, and learning specialists for years, who couldn't determine what was wrong or what to do about it. He hadn't been exposed to drugs, alcohol, or other negative outlets. He loved his parents. Although at times he seemed sullen and anxious about being accepted, he was also a cheerful kid who loved to be home playing with his dog. He was smart, bright even. He had a few awkward friends, just like him. Yet he viewed life as a tug-of-war where everything was negotiable.

His ongoing power struggle with his parents seemed to saturate every aspect of his life. He became verbally and even physically abusive with his parents. He was so strong-willed that he refused any task his parents asked of him, even school. He never trusted a boundary was real. It was clear that although Mack had a high IQ, he lacked the internal resources to actually use his intelligence to benefit his life.

In the wilderness he was funny and playful until it came to any rule or expectation. His small refusals to engage in the program led to more entrenched patterns of shutting down. He assumed a position we came to refer to as "the rock"; he would curl up in a ball with his face to his knees and his hands tucked in. Frequently he did this in his sleeping bag so he had a double layer to his shield—he'd block the whole world out. He would stay in this position most of the day when there was any threat of having to go for a hike or do chores. In the evening he would come out and crack jokes. In addition he had poor self-care skills; although most kids get dirty in the wilderness, Mack resembled Pig Pen. He had a ring of dirt around his neck, coal ash in his hair, black hands, unchanged clothing, and his belongings were in utter disarray. His behavior was extremely frustrating to his peers and the staff.

I sometimes wondered how Mack would handle being alone and lost in the Utah desert. What if he encountered a real-life consequence? Would he stay in his "rock" position and shut down—or would he be hiking for water, collecting firewood, getting organized, and perfecting his fire-making skills? Would he make good choices? Would he rise to the task?

I strongly believed that Mack was behaving this way because all his needs had been met, yet he was not sure how to engage in his own life. He felt a sense of power in opposing others but didn't know how to feel power in his own life, through applying himself. It also seemed like he thrived from having an audience; I was pretty confident that if the rest of the group was gone, Mack would emerge and begin tinkering around the campsite.

In the wilderness the group functions as a whole unit. So if Mack refused to pack up his things and hike to the next spot, then the whole group was stuck. Mack's choices impacted everybody—just like in a family. The intervention that we used in the wilderness was to have the group circle around him and compassionately give him I-feel statements to let him know how he was affecting them. "I feel frustrated when I see you attempt to control the group; this won't get you very far in life." "I feel worried when I see you act this way to get what you want." "I feel sad that we have to stay at this campsite again tonight." "I feel annoyed when I see you act so selfishly."

This approach was used in an attempt to circumvent a power strug-gle. I-feel statements—rather than "you" statements—remove blame and allowed Mack's peers to feel assertive and powerful. The group was not harsh, and the group was not being held hostage to him—the group was simply patient and honest. His peers informed him that his choices affected them.

These interventions occasionally worked because this was the only attention the group gave him. At all other times the group ignored him. When Mack assumed his "rock," the group would do their curriculum: write in their journal, play games, go for short day hikes, and continue on with their own personal growth and group process without him. Conse-quently, he was not getting his daily dose of power, which he had grown to rely on. After an intervention, he'd sporadically agree to hike and par-ticipate for a day, but he was not ready to abandon his deep-set strategy of opposing others and attempting to renegotiate rules.

On a whim one day, when no staff seeming to be looking in his direc-tion, without even slipping on his shoes, he impulsively snuck out behind his shelter, into the juniper trees, up the canyon, and was gone. Mack needed to up the ante in his limit-testing—he was looking for something secure, something real. A few moments had passed before the staff was alerted to Mack's absence.

Many defiant kids attempt to run away and so there is a set protocol to respond to these incidences. After searching through the camp and questioning the other boys, the back-up team was called in and two staff members and I set out to look for Mack. The back-up team arrived shortly and after an hour had passed with still no leads, our alarm started to grow.

In my own anxiety I scrutinized the sandy wash, desperate for a clue. Although there were many boot prints, underneath one I was able discern a print of a large bare foot that undoubtedly was Mack's. He was tall and lanky, and his feet were enormous. I knew we needed to find Mack promptly because the sun was dropping and it would be a cold night in the desert, especially with no socks, shoes, or fire. I didn't want to alert the search team yet, as I feared they would walk all over the wash and trample on my lead. I gently walked along the dry riverbed, stepping on stones, and ahead was able to see a few more footprints. I knew I must be on the right path.

I radioed the team, informing them of my discovery as I made my way up the wash. They soon followed. The sandy wash led up into a small canyon of smooth red rock with beautiful painted stones thrown about. River grass, tamarisk, cottonwood, sage, and juniper grew in clumps in the sand. As I walked, my heart was thumping. A field director was close behind me. After nearly an hour I looked ahead and saw that the canyon opened out into a long vista. We were on a mesa in red-rock country, and I knew there were cliffs around. I followed the barefoot tracks until the sand gave way to sandstone. Once I was on the rock, I had no more markers to follow. Still, I knew there was only one direction for Mack: forward.

I continued on until I came to the cliff's edge. I looked to the left and about thirty feet away Mack was sitting on a rock, wet with tears. I went over and gave him a hug and signaled to the team that I wanted a minute to talk to him. Mack was watching the sun set in an explosion of reds and oranges; he had been sitting on the rock for about two hours now.

"I thought about jumping off, you know." Mack quivered through his tears.

I nodded compassionately. I'd learned through years of work with kids to just listen and not talk in moments like this.

After a long pause, he went on. "But then I realized, I am actually pretty happy. Why would I kill myself? I mean, I have a good life. I have parents who love me. I know I'm pretty smart. I just never do anything—all I do is run away. It's like I am so good at running away that I just keep doing it. All I do is try to escape life. But sitting here and thinking, wow, I'll show them and jump off—but what am I showing you? I actually think I'd be pretty good at making a fire and leading the group. I think I'm going to try now."

"Sounds like you've made some important discoveries. Why don't we get you back to the group before it's dark and have some hot dinner, and you can tell us more at our group session tonight—I know the guys are worried about you."

Sure enough, Mack took responsibility for his actions and expressed his remorse to his peers that night. He admitted that he wanted to change, that his life was not working for him and that he actually thinks living in the wilderness is kind of cool. The next morning, Mack was the first up and got the breakfast fire going, packed up his pack, and led the morning hike. He became a great leader of the boy's group and vowed to never assume his "rock" position again, a vow that he kept. He turned around so completely that he was able to mainstream fairly quickly.

Mack might seem like a dream turnaround case, but upon closer examination, Mack simply lacked limits such that he could apply himself, problem-solve, and develop internal resources. He was getting too much attention and reward for his attention-seeking behaviors, and he faced no real consequences. He moseyed along in his own idiosyncratic way and did whatever he wanted. Although he carried anxiety about whether his power was real, he was not depressed, abused, mistreated, angry, or even suffering from any learning or other disabilities. Mack simply invested his energy and intelligence into his savvy approach to avoiding life. It was all a game; nothing felt real.

Mack, however, was suffering from this approach to life. It may have started as an experiment, but as he continued to flex his "avoid life" muscle, he lost access to his other musculature. Mack was stuck in this pattern. It was his cruise control, always activated. I don't think any of this dawned on Mack until he was face to face with the cliff, at the zenith of his pattern. He just kept moving away from expectations, rules, boundaries, and life duties, while in the process, he was also moving away from friends, family, school, sports, his dog, the comforts of his bed and home, and things he actually enjoyed. When he ran away from camp, he might have initially been seeking attention as he usually did, but when Mack reached the cliff, continuing to move away would mean suicide.

Reaching this limit helped Mack. In fact, some kids only mature when they face real limits, because they never trusted artificial limits in the home, which could be so easily manipulated. Mack woke up out of his denial to actually see what led him to this point; with this, he decided that he wanted to change. How can parents effectively set real limits in the safety of their own home? Many kids who experience wilderness therapy frequently look back at it fondly—how do we bring these concrete forces of nature into our everyday parenting?

Secure Boundaries Reduce Anxiety

Today parents discipline in an ad hoc fashion, negotiating rules and boundaries on a moment-to-moment basis. Coincidentally more children are emotionally immature by age eighteen, and more dependent on their parents. There is also an exponential rise in anxiety disorders in teens; the National Institute for Mental Health reports that *one of every twelve teens suffers from anxiety.*

We must ask ourselves: If there is such a rise in children's anxiety disorders, does this correlate to new parenting practices? When those parents who operate without limits were interviewed in Professor Nelson's study, they reported that availability, intimacy, trust, flexibility, and belief in potential are what they value and identify as producing "great satisfaction" in the parent-child relationship. At the same time, these parents also report ongoing dilemmas and tensions in the home and "fearing that they often got *too* involved in their children's lives, of having difficulty in drawing appropriate limits with respect to disciplinary issues, and of not knowing how to enact trust when the stakes are so very high."

What I have observed in family systems is that this "flexibility" and ability to negotiate in the parent-child relationship is what *increases* anxiety in children. Author and clinical psychologist Wendy Mogel writes in her book *Blessings of a Skinned Knee* that parents today are so invested in having "democracies" within their households that they value a child's self-expression at the expense of a child's sense of security. She writes, "By refusing to be authority figures, these parents don't empower their children, they make them insecure." When adults aren't fully in charge, children become uneasy.

Developmentally, school-aged children are largely concrete in their thinking. The ability to think in more abstract ways does not begin until roughly age eleven, according to developmental psychologist Jean Piaget. Cognitive development is a step process: In children aged two to seven "magical thinking" predominates, while children aged seven to eleven are very logical and concrete in their thinking. It is only after age eleven that children begin abstract reasoning, which involves the abilities to use analogy and metaphor and to analyze and evaluate ideas and thought constructs; these are skills that adults are adept at, not children. Yet parents frequently engage their children as "mini-adults" through nuanced reasoning, assuming their kids understand all the variations of why rules change and shift. For example, some days there is a bedtime and other days there is not. Some days children can run on the sidewalk without shoes, and other days they have to wear shoes. Some days they can get away with shoving their siblings, and other days they can't.

This is highly confusing and anxiety provoking for kids. Parents assume that home is a safe place for kids to "just be," whereas school must be stressful. Yet I would argue that many kids feel relief when there is order, predictability, and set rules, and they feel stress in a home that tends to be chaotic with rules constantly in flux. Many parents tell me that their children are fine in school and then fall apart at home.

When adults attune to the child's developmental stage and create a reliable, concrete environment, this creates a sense of predictability and security and *abates* anxiety. This means giving your son a consequence every time he shoves his sister, even if it is very small. If rules are shifting and changing, kids put a lot of energy into examining and testing the rules, rather than simply accepting them. This can lead to more worrying, more anxiety.

According to developmental psychologists, after age eleven parents can find more success discussing the nuances around rules, as this reflects the child's developmental state. Yet today, many parents try to have these conversations with three-, five-, and eight-year-olds. And it is entirely different negotiating with a teen who has learned to follow rules, as he or she is testing newfound independence and maturity, than negotiating with a child who has never obeyed limits.

Normal Narcissism

Narcissism is normal and developmentally appropriate in small children. However, if it extends into adolescence, it unfortunately can become part of a young person's emerging personality. Psychologist Robert Bly writes in "The Long Bag We Drag Behind Us," "When we were one or two years old we had what we might visualize as a 360-degree personality. Energy radiated out from all parts of our body and all parts of our psyche." The child views him- or herself as the center of the universe—this is natural.

Yet as kids leave toddlerhood, we need to disrupt this normal narcissism. Limits are constraints that allow children to grow up, to be aware of others, to have empathy, to experience disappointment, and to be more connected to the real world. Limits bring us back to reality.

Saying No

For some parents saying no has a finite quality to it—almost like a death—that makes many parents uncomfortable. Saying no is easier when kids ask for something that is beyond a parent's means: a new car, for instance. But many parents even say yes when they can't afford to, or when it goes against their values, because they don't want to disappoint their children. For example, mothers have told me that they have paid for expensive hair extensions, tanning booth sessions, and manicures for their daughters, which directly goes against their beliefs about girls overfocusing on their looks, simply because they could not say no. Other parents have told me they have let their children go to concerts on school nights or stay out late, even though they didn't think it wise. Other parents might cook three separate dinners every night to please each member of the family.

The first noble truth of Buddhism is that suffering is intrinsic to life; similarly our children's sadness or disappointment when we say no is unavoidable. Giving our children what they want is our attempt to avoid perceived suffering, but does it achieve this? Soon the child will "need" something else. Kids need to reconcile their wants and desires with the realities of life—this is part of maturation and moccasin building.

Kids *want* to be in touch with something real. Limits make children feel safe—just like the baby in the womb constantly feels the pressure of the placenta and uterus pushing up against the baby's new skin; this external pressure creates a safe and fertile environment. Toddlers and small children operate better in contained spaces (which grow as the child grows). When kids can master one environment they are ready to roam a larger perimeter, but they still want to know where that fence is—that is safety. As internal resources build, the fence can become the child's yard, neighborhood, town, state, country, and world; with self-mastery and moccasins the child will be equipped to roam.

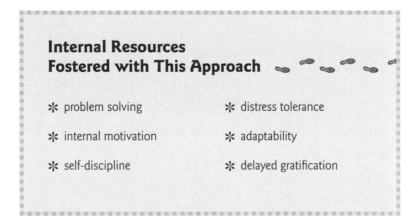

Internal Resources Fostered with This Approach

* problem solving

* internal motivation

* self-discipline

* distress tolerance

* adaptability

* delayed gratification

CHAPTER 6

Skill: Cause-and-Effect Parenting
Connecting Our Kids to the Real World

....

Karma represents the sum total of cause and effect in our lives;
the causes that have made us who we are, the effects we create
moment after moment in response to those causes.
—**Barry Magid,** *Nothing Is Hidden*

....

There are many ways to hold up mirrors for our children and bring cause and effect back into our parenting. Below are some skills that help facilitate this approach.

1. Let Our Children Experience Natural Consequences

Natural consequences happen all the time; we need to let them happen to our children. For example, seeing flowers die in the fall can prompt a discussion about how life starts and ends for everything in the living world. For some children there's a more immediate experience of loss in their lives, such as the death of a pet, a grandparent, or a family member. These events are sad, but ignoring, denying, or fixing such events does not help kids. There are many small griefs that parents tend to skip over. Don't just replace your son's dead goldfish and hope he never notices—it's much better for your child if he loses a fish and experiences a small grief before he encounters the loss of a loved one.

When my children came to understand that we all will die, that even I, their mother, will die, it provoked a discussion about how to live life. I said that though we'll all die none of us knows when it will happen, so we must enjoy each day. I did not say, "I will die in a long, long time," because none of us knows that. Death was not talked about in a scary way; more in a way of acknowledging the natural processes of life. In fact my children, three and five years old at the time, began to talk about death whenever they saw leaves fall from trees, a pumpkin rotting, the place in the backyard where we buried our dog's ashes—these became normal observations of life, not something to cover up. Remember that we can incrementally remove the leather around their feet and allow them to see the world around them in safe, contained ways.

This can be applied to any loss, whether it's divorce, a deployment, a move, or a job termination. We need to listen to kid's emotions and compassionately let them feel.

In everyday life there is loss and disappointment—rather than fixing, parents can moccasin build. In addition to living things dying, many toys and man-made things break. This too is a loss. As an example, there are big tears at my house when balloons break. Yet rather than rushing out to buy a new balloon, I use this opportunity to talk about temporary pleasures and to teach that frequently with joy there is also sadness. Another example is family trips to the bank: sometimes the tellers give stickers and lollipops to my kids, and sometimes they don't. I've told my children, "I am not going to *ask* for a lollipop or sticker; we just need to say 'thank you' if there's a treat." This too has created tears, but once I've acknowledged their feelings, the kids usually move on and hope for the treat next time.

Other natural consequences might be losing personal items such as a book, a cell phone, or a baseball glove. We can't make things "perfect" all the time, and we have to let our kids experience their feelings associated with these losses. Leaving an electronic toy out in the rain might mean that it does not work anymore; this is a natural consequence. We don't need to get alarmed when our kids feel sadness or experience a loss.

Many parents ask when to let kids experience consequences, since when very young they simply do not understand. My answer is to assess the child's age. You can still tell the truth, yet understand that a child between the ages of two and seven may still view it in a magical way, while a seven- to eleven-year-old probably understands consequences in a more concrete, realistic way.

The bottom line is that attempting to rescue our children from natural consequences only takes them away from reality and from cause-and-effect parenting. If your child is not invited to a birthday party, this can be upsetting, yet it is also an opportunity to talk about friendships and social dynamics and to listen and validate your child's feelings. This is a time for empathy, not fixing. When parents get involved and find a way to invite their child to the party it might fix a temporary hurt but may not help with moccasin building when the next rejection comes.

Skill: Do not fix natural consequences; let your children experience them and have their feelings. This is a great opportunity to listen.

Try This: The next time your child is upset or has some disappointment, listen closely and validate the feeling (worry, anger, sadness, etc.). Chances are your child will move on when he or she feels completely heard. Let your children shift on their own. When this happens, they are processing their emotions in the most natural way.

---

2. Give Logical Consequences

Not all actions have clear-cut natural consequences; in these cases, it's up to parents to apply their own logical consequences. Thinking up a logical consequence to fit an occasion requires a little more effort than just letting children experience natural consequences, but it's where parents can be clear and assertive, rather than reactionary. For many families, the created consequence might just be asking your children to go to their rooms if they are disrespectful or defiant. But, if possible, it's good to try to more clearly link behaviors with consequences. Even just talking about logical consequences, in my experience, helps steer behaviors.

For example, in my house we came up with a consequence for when one of my daughters is aggressive toward the other. The offending child has to repair the hurt by reading a story to her sister or making a card for her. What I have observed is that after they settle down they actually love doing this and their energy moves quickly from negative to positive. The goal is not to shame negative behavior, as we are all capable of being aggressive; the goal is to acknowledge feelings and rebuild. An important concept in peacemaking, described in the book *The Anatomy of Peace* by the Arbinger Institute, is the "Change Pyramid." In the Change Pyramid the very tip of the triangle is "dealing with things that are going wrong," which is addressing the aggression or conflict. Yet the bulk of the pyramid is "helping things go right." In the case of siblings we usually put most of our energy into their conflicts, when instead we can put much more energy into building goodwill between them, into diplomacy and peacemaking. If one of my girls comes to me to complain about the other, I usually ask, "Did you tell her how you feel?" I will then hear her say to her sister, "I feel sad and hurt and disrespected when you laugh at me." Although this is never an entirely smooth process, there is usually some acknowledgment that one hurt the other. In these scenarios, I am not intervening or fixing, I am instead encouraging my children to be clear and assertive with each other, and to build the skills to work out their own relationship. This is the fertile soil of the home, where there is conflict on a daily basis. This is where we can choose how we direct our energy.

If a child lies, there can be both natural and logical consequences. A natural consequence is that a parent's trust level has dropped. This is cause and effect: when someone consistently tells us the truth, our trust level goes up, and when someone inconsistently tells the truth, our trust level goes down. I sometimes like to describe trust as a bank account. Each time that a child's words match his actions are like deposits into the "trust bank," and each lie or incongruence is like a withdrawal. This allows us to also establish logical consequences, which allow kids to see that lies are harming themselves, not just their parents. When parents trust their kids they are more likely to let them go to friends' houses or hand their kids the car keys—trust directly improves children's lives.

Still, I have observed many examples of broken trust that do not deter parents from blindly believing their kids. Many kids even use this as a weapon: "You don't even trust your own child!" or "You trust my teacher more than you trust me?" Parents fall for this because every fiber in their bodies *wants* to trust their children—yet parents have to look into the trust bank. Is it empty or full? Parent should trust their children not based on an ideal but on the reality of whether their children are trustworthy. Blind trust can allow kids to engage more deeply in harmful behaviors, until the child runs into some real-life consequence, like a car crash, a police write up, or a suspension. This is why we must apply logical consequences in the home first, even if they're uncomfortable.

A note of caution: We need to set realistic consequences, so we can more easily follow through with them. Many parents threaten grounding their child for a whole week but find themselves unable to follow through. Logical consequences need to be consistently applied in order to be effective. Simple consequences like taking a child's cell phone away for a day is frustrating enough for a kid—and doable for a parent.

The Negative Role of Shame

What differentiates a consequence from a punishment is that the goal of a consequence is not to belittle a child or infringe on the child's dignity—the goal is to have cause and effect. Kids don't feel punished by nature when it gets dark and cold after the sun sets and they are scrambling to organize their belongings without a light; they see it as the natural order of things. Nature does not offer a tone of criticism or disapproval. Yet frequently when we employ consequences, our emotional reactions are still present and written on our faces or heard in our tone. These can include disappointment or even withholding and can make the consequence into a punishment. How can we give consequences that seem as natural as the sunset—without any emotional loading?

Today there is considerable psychological awareness regarding the negative effects of name-calling, belittling, or humiliating our children, but there is a more subtle method of shaming on the rise. Psychologist Richard Weissbourd reports in *The Parents We Mean to Be* that the emphasis on being "perfect," "happy," or even "fine" sets up unrealistic expectations. When kids don't feel happy all the time, they feel that something must be wrong with them. Parents work so hard to create perfect environments and fix disappointments they become frustrated when their kids aren't happy, and kids can sense this. Weissbourd writes, "Feelings such as anger, jealousy, and even shame itself can become sources of shame."

It's important to distinguish between guilt and shame. Guilt is associated with doing something wrong, something that violates one's values:

showing disrespect, lying, yelling, cheating, and stealing. It's good, in fact, to feel guilty about these actions because it means we care about ourselves and others. Shame, however, is associated with feeling bad about one's self, not about one's actions. Individuals who experience a great deal of shame frequently don't care about others, because they have an acute feeling of their own unworthiness.

Today, overt shaming may have largely been left in previous generations, but subtle shaming is alive and present, though harder to flush out. Many young adults who show up in therapists' offices today do not report problems with their parents as in previous generations. They say, "I had great parents, very committed, and I am still very close to them." Instead, they feel that they are the problem—"something is wrong with me." Kids today are only allowed to feel happy; they feel guilty or bad when they are worried, sad, anxious, frustrated, and so on.

For many kids today, the full spectrum of positive and negative emotions are not mirrored, heard, or validated by their parents. The issue is the same for whoever walks into a therapist's office—individuals need help accessing and experiencing their emotions. Whether parents are critical or devoted, both can disrupt a child's ability to feel.

I recently taught a course at Middlebury College during which I wrote on the board thirty "feeling words." I asked the students to do a "feelings check," where they simply had to pick a word that most closely matched how they felt at that moment. The students said it was a strange yet refreshing exercise, because they never normally stopped and identified what they felt. The students were allowed to see that they usually manage their emotions on a more unconscious level. I then asked them to imagine that the thirty words were colors and to pick a color associated with their feeling. Did the color—yellow, grey, blue, purple—allow them to experience the emotion—worry, reluctance, frustration, contentment—differently? Was there less judgment, less labels of "good" or "bad"? Most admitted to a strong inner judgment of any negative emotion such as sadness, worry, frustration. There was a marked sense in the group that they should only acknowledge positive emotions.

It's important for parents to be aware of subtle messages they may be sending in their cause-and-effect parenting. We are all capable of making poor choices, and our children are no different. Instead of emotionally loading our responses and judging our children, we simply have to hold our children accountable. If my child exhibits some egregious behavior and then receives a consequence, we don't need to keep bringing it up and reminding her of it; we can all move on. Allowing children to be accountable for their poor behaviors or choices can actually free them, rather than adding to a feeling of guilt.

We have to give consequences in an even-keeled way. I've learned that my daughters are more upset by my disappointed tone than by a consequence itself. Thus, I try to give my kids consequences in a very matter-of-fact manner and remind them that they have a choice; then I can detach from the outcome. So for example, if my kids decide they hate something on their dinner plate, I tell them they can't have any dessert or other food without trying it, but it's up to them. In this way, applying logical consequences can free us up as parents.

Being Playful

Logical consequences can also be creative and fun. In my years of work with teens in wilderness settings, I have even found that eliciting their input allows them to feel part of the process. Astonishingly, kids often come up with harsher consequences than I might have imagined. For example, in some wilderness programs kids can earn a camp chair. So a student might say, "I will lose my camp chair for a week if I am defiant, because I am not setting a good example for my peers, and my chair is a symbol of making good choices," when I might have only taken the chair away for one day.

Consequences can be transformational for our children if we include them in the decision-making and problem-solving processes. Some families can even set consequences for adults—this supports the notion that we all have to be accountable to each other. So for example, my husband and I pay our kids a quarter if we say a swear word. This allows our kids to know that we also have to be accountable. For myself, I frequently take time-outs if I am getting too frustrated with them and realize I need to go to my room for a few minutes. Kids are not the only ones who have to work on their behavior; parents getting involved offers a way to model that we all have opportunities to make healthy and unhealthy choices—they are not "bad" for making an unhealthy choice. We are all in the process of building our moccasins.

Skill: Use creativity to come up with appropriate logical consequences that fit each incident that arises. Value these small struggles in the home because they prepare kids for cause and effect in the real world.

Try This: Ask your child to come up with a consequence for his problematic behavior and ask him to follow through with it on his own. This will build trust, accountability, and integrity.

---

3. Positive Consequences, or Giving Rewards

Just as a poor choice should be met with a negative consequence, positive choices often yield positive outcomes. Natural positive consequences happen as a result of a child making healthy choices that can bring more trust and more freedom. Yet when working with troublesome behaviors, sometimes attaching a reward can be another way to steer a child toward healthier choices.

Giving kids an incentive to examine their behaviors can also foster the maturation process. For example when a child has an anger outburst, such as yelling, screaming, threatening, and slamming doors, parents can strategically address the anger using an I-feel statement attached to a plan. "I feel powerless when you become so angry. I cannot stop your anger or control you; only you can control you. What if I reward you for learning how to control your outbursts on your own? You're still entitled to your angry feelings; you just can't express them in a destructive way. If you can consecutively and appropriately manage your anger for a whole week, I will give you $10 for your favorite candy store. It's just an idea; what do you think? If you blow up before the week ends, we'll start again. It's your choice if you want to try it."

Although many parents might scoff at this idea, many kids would jump on this. Even if the child is managing his anger for the wrong reasons (i.e., candy), he is trying on a new behavior: self-control. This new behavior rewires the brain, as now a new signal is associated with anger: refraining and calming down. These are enormously positive actions for a child with an anger problem. In treatment we often use the phrase "fake it until you make it." It doesn't matter if the child is managing anger for genuine reasons or for candy; the child is still working to break an ingrained behavioral pattern, such as a tantrum. This will only serve the child.

After a parent spends $10, $20, or perhaps $30 on candy for solid weeks without anger, that is money well spent. This doesn't need to continue forever. After a while a parent can say, "You've really shown me that you know how to manage your anger. Moving forward we're not going to reward you with candy anymore, but I now have faith that you know how to control yourself. Now the reward is a newfound maturity and more self-control."

An important thing to remember is that the parent cannot be more invested than the child in earning the reward. If the parent is too focused on the child earning the candy, the child will likely not follow through. The child has to feel internally motivated. This can be hard work for the whole family, yet it is important to remember that we would much rather kids have this struggle safely in the home than out in the real world.

Skill: Shift the negative-consequence tone around and think of positive consequences for kids who learn to manage their emotions on their own in healthy and productive ways. For instance, we frequently give kids treats when they are upset to make them happy. What if we gave a reward instead to a child who refrained from anger and calmed herself on her own?

Try This: Ask your child what he would like to earn for better managing his anger—or better organizing his morning routine— consistently for a week. This is how the world works: emotional self-management and organizational skills tend to be rewarded in life.

4. I-Feel Statements

I-feel statements are another way to hold up mirrors for our children about their behavior.

Our feelings give kids information about how they impact us. This communication is not done in a blaming way but in a matter-of-fact, clear way. "I feel upset and sad when you lied about where you went after school." Relationships involve two people and if we want our children to be mindful about others' feelings and emotions we have to bring our feelings into the parent-child relationship. This skill was described in detail in part 1, so feel free to look back and freshen up.

> **Skill:** When feeling upset by your child, tune in to your emotions and ask yourself exactly what you're feeling. Review I-feel statements and then tell your child how you feel, using that format.
>
> **Try This:** Ask your child to use an I-feel statement if she is shutting you out or making "you statements." Validate what your child feels even if she is mad at you. I would much rather my children tell me they are mad at me than have a door slammed in my face or have them retreat away from me.

Talking about consequences in daily life lets kids see consequences all around them. For example, seeing a police car pull over a speeder tells kids the consequences for driving too fast; returning library books late incurs a late fee; discussing the paucity of jobs for people without a college degree lets kids know the necessity of education. These are realities in life, so rather than hovering over and steering our kids we can educate them and let them make their own choices. When kids make their own choices they are more likely to be invested in their own life.

Many parents tell me consequences don't work because their children don't care about losing privileges, yet those same children work hard to earn and keep privileges in therapeutic programs. Almost every child cares about something, whether it's a computer game, a cell phone, or social time—even a camp chair. Kids have just become adept at reading their parents' cues and responding accordingly to win a power struggle. Remember: when kids are gaining power in the home, they are less likely to want to gain a sense of personal power in the real world. And truthfully it does not matter if parents think the consequence is "working"—what matters is following through and being consistent, so that the child learns the lesson of the law of cause and effect.

PART III

Boulders:
Obstacles on the Trail

CHAPTER 7
The Parent's Trail

Cooper

Cooper tragically lost his mother to cancer when he was only thirteen years old. His older brother had just left for college, and Cooper was left home alone with his grieving and brokenhearted father. Today Cooper remembers the heavy silences in the house, the creaks of his father's chair in the den, his habit of tiptoeing around the house to pretend he was invisible. His father was always emotionally distant, so to have his mother—the source of warmth and joy in his life—taken away from him was an insurmountable loss. He remembers feeling overcome with pain, with nowhere to turn. One day after months of feeling shut down, he worked up the courage to speak to his father about it.

Cooper walked gently into his father's den and sat down on the couch while his father read the newspaper. His dad turned the paper down, looked at Cooper, and then resumed his evening read. They were good at silences. After wringing his hands for a long while, Cooper cleared his throat and, looking at the back of the newspaper, said out loud: "I miss her so much."

Cooper expected to feel relief, but instead a cold sweat ran across his skin. He soon heard his father crinkle up the *Times* and throw it on the carpet. "You miss her so much? Well, at least you have your life ahead of you; I have nothing left." Panicked, Cooper got up and left the room.

After this gamble with vulnerability, Cooper learned to never mention his mother to his father again.

This event imprinted so strongly on his psyche that Cooper swore to himself that he would never allow his children to ever feel alone—*ever*. He emphatically believed that someone could have taken his pain away when he was a grieving teen, if only someone had been there who cared. He knew he would be that caring father for his kids.

Cooper and his wife Karen had three daughters. And although they never spoke openly about it, Lizzie, the youngest, age 8, was a source of enormous stress for the family. She was always going against the grain, resisting, showing irritability, and being obstinate. Moreover, after struggling for years in school, she was diagnosed with a nonverbal learning disability.

Cooper felt an overwhelming sadness for Lizzie, and true to his convictions, he was unrelenting in his attempts to take away her pain. Her diagnosis elicited an even stronger effort to anticipate her needs; he worried, "Is she processing information incorrectly? Maybe she doesn't fully understand what others are saying." Thus, whenever Lizzie expressed or implied any upset, Cooper was there to the rescue. He became an expert at reading her nonverbal cues. He felt he could fill in her gaps. Lizzie didn't even need to say anything, she could just pout, look a certain way, or show frustration, and Cooper was jolted into action—making her a new dinner, helping her with her homework, finishing her chore, cleaning her room, and so on.

Parents' Boulders

Many parents are so focused on all the boulders and obstacles on their child's trail they lose sight of their *own* boulders. Though we might be otherwise functional adults who have jobs, commitments, and responsibilities, many of us stop our own growth processes when we have children, instead investing ourselves in our child's growth. However, wanting to provide for our children and raise them in the best possible way also means continuing to grow ourselves. All relationships are made up of two people, and in the parent-child relationship, parents also need to invest in their side of the equation. This of course can be very challenging, as most parents have their child's side of the equation under the microscope.

When a parent observes a child experiencing emotional pain, it can remind the parent of his or her own pain from childhood. If a father has simply stuck his head in the sand all these years to avoid seeing and feeling his pain—however large or small—it frequently can ambush him when he's confronted with his child's struggles. None of this happens at a conscious level; instead a father quickly reacts to fix the son's struggle to avert the feeling of failure he had as a kid. In this way, childhood pain can rear its ugly head in our parent-child relationship patterns.

Parents are their children's emotional role models—whether they like it or not. We cannot ask our children to do something that we're not also willing to do ourselves. We can't allow a child to stay with her own sadness if we're quick to look for an exit when we're sad. To model effectively, we need to let ourselves feel our own sadness, disappointment, frustration, anxiety—and stay with these emotions without exaggeration or shutting down. We need to demonstrate that we're willing to feel and hear others' emotions, even in a conflict—rather than cutting ourselves off from people or "fixing" them. We need to be accountable for our shortcomings and repair mistakes. It is much harder to simply stay present and open to our children than to engage autopilot responses. Staying with the unknown is building moccasins; staying in automatic patterns is an effort to stay in control and build a cushion around us.

> ► When a parent's anxiety triggers an emotional roller coaster, this is what kids are learning—how to let anxiety spiral.
>
> ► When parents snap when they are overwhelmed, this is what kids are learning—how to lash out.
>
> ► When parents refuse to feel or stay present in their lives, this is what kids are learning—the emotional shutdown.

Relax; we all have negative habits. And of course, many children are enormously different from their parents. Yet, in any scenario, parents can still model how to work with emotions, share feelings, stay with discomfort, be vulnerable, set limits, take responsibility, repair conflict, validate feelings, and even embrace uncertainty. But before we can do this we have to be self-aware and know our automatic responses to our emotional content.

Automatic Responses

Automatic responses are part of a parent's emotional response system, which stems from the parent's personal story. In treating children, adolescents, and young adults, the focus is always on the child's struggle. However, we all know that children are not raised in vacuums; they are raised in one or more parents' emotional stories. We cannot pretend that these emotional responses and stories don't exist. In fact, they are there loud and clear, for better or for worse, in our interactions with our children.

Highlighting these automatic responses is critical to successfully examining parent-child relationship patterns and allowing new outcomes in the parent-child relationship to emerge.

Cooper

Cooper, described in the story above, was perpetually solving problems for his daughter; he couldn't help himself. Any struggle of hers, expressed or not, he was anticipating, researching, planning, and fixing. He worked tirelessly behind the scenes. Yet he had no idea that he was anxious or that he was engaging in these behaviors. All of this was unexamined because at a core place he felt that this is what parents do. Cooper admitted he could not imagine not trying to help his daughter when she struggled. What would happen if he refrained from all his rescuing efforts and instead let his daughter problem-solve alone?

When Cooper came to examine *his* automatic parenting response he began to look into his personal story. He came to see that the idea of abstaining from helping his daughter created a panicky feeling for him because he had had no one to help him through the painful period of losing his mother. Cooper assumed being a good father meant never letting his daughter face something alone. Although his intentions seemed logical and benign on one level, Cooper began to see that his behaviors were mostly driven by his anxiety from his childhood. This awareness upset him. He thought: "Am I helping her or trying to protect myself?" Realizing how confusing this was, Cooper felt compelled to hold himself back and only assist his daughter when he knew for sure he wasn't motivated by an anxious response system that he had unconsciously cultivated over the years.

Cooper also began to see that although his intentions were genuine, his daughter was deeply dependent on him and did not know how to solve problems on her own, which actually made her *less* capable of dealing with her learning disability. He had disrupted her emotional maturation process. He also began to admit how demanding, impatient, and irritable she could be. Refraining from rescuing was challenging for him and his daughter alike, yet with time this led to new outcomes and allowed his daughter to resume her emotional growth.

Now Cooper only helps his daughter if she explicitly asks for it and if the request seems reasonable, because she is then taking some responsibility in getting help. Though this was difficult at first, he noticed when he stopped tirelessly working on her behalf that he had new energy to apply in his own life, which he devoted to becoming fit again—this too helped restore balance in the parent-child relationship.

Cooper's Automatic Response:
Rescuing his daughter from struggle in order to manage his own anxiety.

Linda

Linda always, no matter what the circumstances, threw a blanket of sympathy on her son's behaviors, however egregious they were. Linda had found her own mother to be harsh, so she was always eager to listen to her son's explanations and see his side. When he shut down, lied, threatened, or was disrespectful, there was always some excuse for his behavior. The result of this automatic response was that Linda quickly lost sight of what she was feeling. Was she frustrated when he shut down, hurt when he was disrespectful, and angry when he threatened or lied? What was Linda's personal story behind this imbalance?

When her son entered therapy, Linda was asked by the therapist why her son acted out. Linda's assumption was that her son was in pain; this was why she always went right to comforting and fixing. When asked what *she* felt, Linda went blank. That was not something that she had access to; she was too busy focusing on anticipating others' needs and feelings.

With time and the guidance of a therapist, Linda discovered that *she* was in pain, related to losses in her own childhood. In truth she no idea what her son felt; she'd never asked him. Linda's emotional response system came from her personal story: she was raised in a family in which both parents had strong personalities, influenced by alcohol, to which she had to adapt. Linda saw their feelings and worked hard to please her parents. No one saw, mirrored, or validated her emotions. She never really knew what she felt, and when she did feel down, she turned to self-criticism.

As Linda began to tune in to her own emotions, she noticed for the first time that she felt not only frustrated but angry at her son's ongoing disrespect. Anger was hard to identify and admit to, as she'd never had an awareness of feeling it before. However, this was a turning point not only for Linda, but for her son as well. She told him in their next therapy session, "Sweetie, I love talking to you and your feelings are very important to me; however, I will not tolerate any more disrespect in your communication. The next time that you are disrespectful I will end the conversation by letting you know that I can't listen or talk unless you speak to me differently."

Linda had to follow through on this and had to cut many phone calls and conversations short. She felt sad about this, but she also knew she was not doing him any favors by allowing him to be disrespectful or emotionally manipulative. Awareness of her automatic response led her to realize her own anger and frustration, and this led to Linda setting her first boundary and holding her son accountable. This was hard but also deeply gratifying. As Linda became more consistent in her parenting, she also felt more clarity and strength. This insight and behavioral shift restored equilibrium in the parent-child relationship. In return her son did speak more respectfully to her, because that was what she required.

Linda's Automatic Response:
Denying her own emotions to care for others.

Paul

Paul comes home and yells. He points out that the house is a mess. He doesn't understand why his son always has his headphones on or is in his room with the door shut. "Why is he blocking me out? I'm at work all day—I want to hang out with him and shoot some hoops. Is that too much to ask? He doesn't even acknowledge me." Paul is more and more frustrated and feels he lacks any significance in his son's life. Yet this frustration only seems to deepen the father-son divide. What is Paul's personal story? Why is he so angry?

Paul was raised by a single mom. Ever since he became a father, he made a commitment to himself that he would play an important role in his son's life. Yet he admitted to feeling powerless and confused when it came to parenting. Paul knew that lecturing, advising, and pushing his son into activities was not working. He reluctantly admitted, "Truthfully, I don't even know what a father 'should' be doing, because I didn't have one; I'm just trying to be there for him."

With his awareness of what he wanted most—a relationship—Paul said to his son, "In my head I keep telling myself how lucky you are to have a dad that comes home every day that loves you, and I get frustrated when you don't appreciate it. But I'm realizing that that is my story, not yours. You probably think, 'I have an angry dad.' So now that I'm more aware of what I feel, I want to ask, what would you like to do together? Can we set aside some time together every night when I come home? That would mean so much to me." Awareness of Paul's automatic responses led to new outcomes and closeness with his son.

Paul's Automatic Response:
Projecting his stored anger and sadness onto his son as a result of his lack of relationship with his own father.

Congruent Communication

Kids are experts from birth at reading their parents' faces, emotions, gestures, and cues. The subject they have been studying the most in their life is *you*. When parents come to understand their own emotional states and reactions and realize they have choices, they can model to their children that they too have choices. They can slam a door, or they can take a deep breath. They can lash out, or they can be assertive. They can play the victim, or they can hold their child accountable. Parents can keep piling up negatives in response to feelings, or they can just stay with one negative emotion and feel it fully, until it subsides and drifts away.

When parents become aware of their feelings, they become more *congruent*: their verbal communication matches their nonverbal communication. So many parents say they are "fine," yet all their nonverbal cues indicate anger, anxiety, tension, or disappointment. This is tremendously confusing for kids. Kids are reading their parents' nonverbal cues yet hearing contrasting words. Child psychiatrist Daniel Siegel writes in *Parenting From the Inside Out*:

> If verbal and nonverbal signals communicate different messages—are not congruent—the overall message will be unclear and confusing. We are getting two different and conflicting messages at once. Suppose a mother is sad and her daughter, picking up the nonverbal signals asks, "Mommy, what's wrong? Did I do something to make you sad?" and with a forced smile the mother replies, "Oh no, honey, I'm not sad, everything is just fine." The child will feel confused because of the double message.

However, when parents say, "I'm feeling sad about grandma's health," or "I'm feeling angry because you showed disrespect," or "I feel anxious when you struggle," or "I'm sad that I didn't have a relationship with my dad"—kids can relate to this. When communication is congruent it is straightforward and makes sense. This brings relief.

Congruent communication also reminds children that parents aren't always "fine," which teaches them that it's okay to not always be "fine."

When kids feel a range of emotions, with intense or strong feelings mixed in, they may feel that something is wrong with them if they don't see this range reflected in their parents. Feelings are central to the human experience. Normalization of feelings is a terrific way to minimize the subtle shame that results when a child feels something is "wrong" with him or her. Feelings come and go; we don't need to get alarmed about them.

Parents, however, don't need to overstep the boundaries around feelings. For example, an upset mother could say, "Sweetie, I'm just feeling sad because I had a disagreement with Dad; sometimes adults have trouble working things out too, not just kids." This parent is not pulling the child into the conflict; this parent is being honest, open, and congruent. Kids see their parents' disagreements whether they are explosive, passive-aggressive, or simply avoiding each other. When parents share openly, with appropriate boundaries in place, parental arguing is not as scary for kids. A mother could say, "I have a feeling we'll work it out, but right now I'm feeling sad. How are you feeling?" Conflict is part of healthy relationships and healthy families, so we don't need to work so hard to avoid it; we simply need the right tools and techniques.

In fact, I think the concept that parents are the biggest emotional objects in their children's lives is quite thrilling (and daunting). Parents are actually terribly significant. Rather than feeling powerless in your child's life, realize that your child is watching you daily, if not hourly. Parents can pause, refrain, and stay with discomfort and anxiety. If you become aware of your automatic responses from your personal story, chances are you are restoring more balance and equanimity in the home. You are modeling the moccasin-building process.

Equanimity is a stable and composed state of mind, undisturbed by emotions or events. The Buddhist term for equanimity is *upekkha*, meaning "to look over," which refers to the ability to see without being caught by what we see. In parenting you could say equanimity is stepping off your child's emotional rollercoaster—remaining calm, despite whatever behavior your child chooses. Consistent, collected responses from their parents create safety and reliability for kids and allow them to form their own independent thoughts.

Discovering and Addressing Your Automatic Response

A starting point for all parents who want to become more conscious of their automatic emotional responses is a feelings journal. Simply jot down one or more emotions a minimum of three times a day. This is not an exercise to vent, lash out, identify yourself as a victim, or to blame others; it is simply an exercise to identify and record your feelings. For example, at 7:45 AM you might be sad, tired, or worried about the coming day. This journal is only about YOU.

I feel:	
Morning:	
Noon:	
Night:	

The first objective of this exercise is to *identify emotions*: sad, worried, scared, angry, expectant, proud, content, etc. Many parents who are enmeshed, overinvolved, or struggling with their children have no idea what they are feeling—they are too focused on their child's (or other person's) emotion or behavior. When parents stop and tune in to their own emotions, they take a giant step forward to create more balance and awareness in the parent-child relationship. Feelings journals are great for emotional literacy in the home.

The second objective is to *identify behaviors*: gaining an understanding of your behavioral patterns, of the way you act out your underlying emotions. For example, if a parent is anxious and jumps into an action, there is a direct connection between anxiety and the action. Yet many parents are not even aware of their deeply entrenched patterns with their children. Often this critical piece of information—self-awareness—is missing, which contributes to stuck parent-child patterns. When parents grow in their self-awareness, they understand their own behaviors at a deeper level.

The third objective is *changing behavior*. Once you're aware of what you feel and what you do, you have a choice whether you continue in the same pattern or not. When parents clearly *see* their own behavior, and they do not like what they see, this is a big motivator to change.

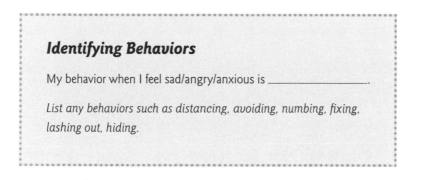

Identifying Behaviors

My behavior when I feel sad/angry/anxious is _____.

List any behaviors such as distancing, avoiding, numbing, fixing, lashing out, hiding.

Changing Behavior

Do I want to frantically spiral my anxiety, or can I sit with my discomfort for even one minute and let it settle? Do I want to cheer up my daughter and attempt to make her happy, or can I just listen and validate her sadness? Do I want to wall myself off and do chores or go on my computer, or can I allow myself to feel the tension in my body and take a few slow breaths? Do I want to yell at the people I love the most, or can I take five minutes to decompress before I walk in the door and say anything? Should I make excuses for my daughter again, or can I set a limit and tell her that disrespect is never acceptable communication?

The first step of behavior change for parents is simply *refraining*. When parents refrain they are disrupting their automatic, habitual response. This means pausing from any action: yelling, isolating, going on the computer, fixing, and so on. I read a parenting article once that used the language of "tying yourself to a mast." Sometimes we are so caught up in a moment that we can't simply pause; we have to tie ourselves to a metaphorical mast. Doing so gives us the opportunity, no matter how fraught the moment, to ask, "What am I feeling right now?"

When parents take a moment to catch their breath and evaluate the situation clearly, they realize they are not trapped. Choices create autonomy, empowerment, and self-direction. This is exactly the process we want kids to go through. We want them to make new choices. This refraining and holding yourself back is essential to letting your child take a step forward.

This self-awareness can also allow parents to connect the dots to their personal story, upbringing, or unresolved feelings from childhood; parents can own their boulders. After all, our emotional reactions come from somewhere. This self-discovery on the parents' end pays dividends when parents know how to diffuse automatic triggers and engage their children from a place of clarity.

Practicing New Behaviors

The new behavior I want to practice is _____.

List any methods such as refraining, pausing, taking a deep breath, walking around the block, or allowing yourself to feel your emotions without reactivity.

Children Hold Up Mirrors for Us

One day when I was rushing around, trying to get organized, trying to get everything in the car, and tearing out of our driveway to get where we needed to go, I realized about five minutes into our drive that I had forgotten something and had to turn around and speed back home. I complained out loud, "I try so hard to be organized, and I just can't do it." My oldest daughter said to me, "Mom, when you rush, you forget about yourself." Wow. She never studied Buddhism, but at that moment she was like a wise master, giving me spot-on advice. She intuitively knew that I'd left my self, my breath, and my self-awareness. I was responding to anxious stimuli and expressing it through rushing.

Our children see our patterns whether we like it or not; we can't hide from them. We need to listen to and value our children's feedback, even if it stings sometimes. It's good when our children hold us accountable, because then we can hold them accountable. At the end of a day, for a family to work well, all the individuals need to answer to each other. Our children know us emotionally and psychically—so it is best for us to keep owning our "shadows," habits, and automatic patterns. This will more likely reduce our feelings of being emotionally ambushed.

Whether you experienced pain in your childhood that you bring into your parenting today, or you simply are a committed parent who tries to make everything "perfect," it's best to be conscious of your automatic responses and own them. Emotional growth for parents is ongoing and needs to be worked on and modeled to kids. In *Nothing Is Hidden*, Zen teacher Barry Magid writes about the dangers of "an unhealthy devotion to others at the expense of one's own legitimate emotional and physical needs—a parody of compassion that I have called *vowing to save all beings minus one.*"

Parents must discern whether their responses to their children are rooted in "rescuing" and solving problems or in deep empathy and validation. When we respond with equanimity, when we own our own boulders, we don't have to interfere with our children's good days or bad days. When we are comfortable with our pain, we will not jump when our kids hit a bump. We can't control everything in our children's experience. And most importantly, *we have to stop moving their boulders for them.*

Assignments:

1) Keep a feelings journal, noting a minimum of three feelings a day. Stick with it for a minimum of one week. Do this knowing that before you attune to your child it's best to know what you are feeling.

2) What patterns did you notice?

3) Have you gained awareness of your behavioral responses to your emotions? For example: when anxious, do you jump to action to solve your child's problem?

4) What choices do you have as a parent to have new outcomes with your child? What can you control?

5) How can you make your verbal and nonverbal communication more congruent?

6) How can you model emotional maturity for your child more effectively?

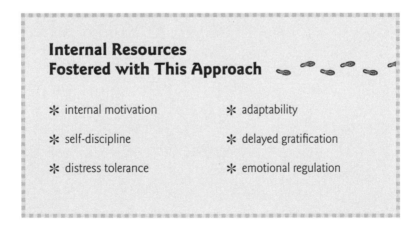

Internal Resources
Fostered with This Approach

✻ internal motivation   ✻ adaptability

✻ self-discipline   ✻ delayed gratification

✻ distress tolerance   ✻ emotional regulation

CHAPTER 8

The Child's Trail

....

Look at children. Of course they may quarrel, but generally speaking they do
not harbor ill feelings as much or as long as adults do. Most adults have the
advantage of education over children, but what is the use of an education
if they show a big smile while hiding negative feelings inside?
—His Holiness The Dalai Lama, *Imagine All the People*

....

Moccasin building can *only* happen on your child's trail, not on some
merged family path. Their trail is out of your domain. Kids have to have
a sense that they are the stewards of their own lives. Moccasin building
happens when a daughter is aware of her own feelings and she is able to
sit with discomfort. Or when a son is able to tap into his own problem-
solving abilities and experiences the outcomes of his choices. With these
skills, kids learn through trial and error to navigate the rocks and boulders on their paths. Parents, however, can be guides by highlighting and
validating feelings, effectively framing and following through with consequences, and encouraging problem solving and emotional regulation.
Parents can teach or suggest ways to navigate the boulders and rocks, but
they can't do it for their children. Kids ultimately have to learn how to
navigate their own way through their terrain.

Most important of all, parents have to stop being the child's trail main-
tenance crew. Parents have to stop moving the child's boulders off the
trail and stop laying down the leather over all their sharp rocks. Many
parents today assume responsibility for their child's life trail; yet this is
backbreaking work and is not sustainable. Don't forget the lesson from
the last chapter; parents have enough of their own boulders.

Moreover, parents simply cannot always be there to control or foresee every obstacle. It's a rude awakening to many overmanaging parents when they learn that their child has been living a secret life away from them. I have heard stories from many hovering parents who think they are in control only to discover that their children have ventured off their leather padding. One parent who thought her son was not even capable of going to school was surprised to find out he decided to hop a bus to visit a friend a few states away. One father learned that his "ultra-mature, high-achieving, got-everything-together daughter" was actually living a dual life, harboring a pot addiction and drug business to support her habit.

This role of trail manager is not helping your child. Your child's life is his or her responsibility. How do parents shift away from trail managing and toward trail guiding? We can't control all the rocks and boulders, but we can do our best to instill healthy problem-solving skills and internal resources.

Natural Problem Solvers

I believe children are incredibly adept at navigating obstacles, if they are only given the opportunity. Kids may not always do this at home, but they do this in the wilderness. We are all born with these skills—it's how we have survived through millennia. Even children with quirks, intense dispositions, sensitive temperaments, or attention-deficit problems still have natural problem-solving abilities. The question is whether we let them hone and develop these inborn skills. I like to think of the ability to solve problems as a muscle; it has to be used, strengthened, and refined. We have to *ask* children to problem-solve. Doing so is a gesture of empowerment and signifies that we trust their intelligence.

I once saw, in a book that discussed parenting paradigms, a picture of an eighteen-month-old in the Amazon wielding a machete, as this is how the tribespeople navigate their dense jungles. Though a shocking image, it represented to me how differently children across the world are asked to participate in their families and communities. Exceedingly safety focused, we in the West may hand a four-year-old a dull butter knife to cut a banana or spread peanut butter on bread—but a machete? The question arises: under the guise of safety, how much do we prevent our kids from growing up and engaging and participating in family life? In Africa a five-year-old girl may help with tending babies, while a five-year-old boy may join in with the hunting expeditions. Many Western kids today, on the other hand, are still largely engaged in play and entertainment—not household participation—until much older. These examples from different cultures illustrate that our young children are capable of more than we think.

Even if we're not ready to give our preschoolers proper chores, we can still ask them to pick up their toys and begin to solve problems. If there is a conflict between siblings we can ask them, "What is the best way to solve this?" If a child feels rushed every morning to get out to daycare, a parent can ask, "What do you think we can do differently?" We can even ask, "What do we need to pack in your backpack today?" We can more fully engage them in their lives; it's amazing the ingenuity kids come up with if we simply ask them to participate. This leads to empowerment and increased self-esteem.

While on a time-out in her room, a mother hears her four-year-old give her doll a "consequence" for hitting. She hears her daughter say, "Baby, it is never okay to hit. You sound upset; can you tell me what you're feeling? You need to take a break in your crib." This form of play, modeled after the parent, allows the child to process and integrate her own time-out. Parents can even ask, "What happens if your dolly doesn't listen to you, or hits you?" Kids begin to connect the dots; if it's not okay for the doll to hit, it's not okay for them to hit either. When we let children feel and also let them face limits, they are quite imaginative at solving their own problems, processing their feelings, and moving on.

A seven-year-old struggled with a disruptive boy at school every day. She despaired, "He always says annoying stuff and causes problems." When asked by her teacher what she could do to help her situation, she replied that she wasn't sure. Her teacher asked her to think about it. The second grader experimented each day and discovered that when she included him in her outdoor play at recess, he was nicer in the classroom. She realized that though he may have anger, he really wants friends. When a child's obstacle (in this case, the disruptive boy) isn't simply removed by an adult, he or she can learn to work with it and will feel a sense of mastery. Many parents want their children to have a perfect school environment, but obstacles frequently provide tremendous lessons and social learning.

In a Montessori classroom, there is only one of every classroom mate-rial—one puzzle map of a specific country, one set of counting beads, and so on. When there are twenty children in the classroom, kids have to negotiate and cooperate to determine which child uses which material on a daily basis. Though potentially frustrating, this arrangement cultivates internal resources such as delayed gratification, frustration tolerance, self-regulation, and problem solving.

A twelve-year-old felt rejected by a friend who did not invite him to his party. He was quite sad, and his mother validated the feeling: "That is upsetting, to not be included." She then asked, "How would you like to solve this problem?" After some time thinking, the boy actually came back with an elaborate plan, which he was quite excited about. He decided that instead of going to the party he wanted to work on the tree house he was building, and maybe if he feels like it, he would invite that friend over when it was finished. Kids can process their own feelings and solve their own problems, if we let the boulders stay on their trail.

A sixteen-year-old really wanted to go to a concert that was in another state. She realized that her parents wouldn't let her go, so she became depressed. Her parents asked her what she could do to solve her situation. She at first said, "Nothing," and became more and more dramatic. Her dad said, "Well, if you're interested in problem solving, we're interested in listening." She went on her computer and realized that she would be visiting her grandparents in Florida with her family in March and her favorite band was playing only thirty minutes away from there. She asked her parents if this was a possibility and they said yes.

Kids feel empowered and in charge of their lives if we let them solve their own problems. When we let the boulder stay on our daughter's trail, or the problem stay in our son's lap, they process their emotions in more fluid ways, rather than getting stuck and looking for an escape or for us to fix it. Many kids that go toward drugs and deception actually use quite a bit of intelligence and savvy to go around the rules. How do we let kids use this natural intelligence to pursue healthy goals? We have to ask them to be problem solvers. We have to let go of control and invite in the unknown. I remember when my young daughter wanted to empty the dishwasher. I was reluctant at first, since I didn't know where she would put everything, yet she stacked bowls in a cabinet drawer and actually got them all to fit in a way that I was never able to before. She solved the problem better than I had.

We have to value and uphold family participation if we want kids to engage in family life. One problem is that so many parents in the professional middle class—who are successful in their careers—are skilled problem solvers. Many parents' default settings are to instantly search for solutions. Many parents have told me that every day in their professions they are solving problems, managing people (staff), and anticipating and managing risk. When they come home, they employ the same skills with their kids. Parents need to refrain. Kids aren't getting stuck when we leave a problem in their lap; they're learning how to stay with struggle and discomfort and how to self-manage and self-regulate. This process creates the opportunity to boost confidence, self-esteem, and self-mastery. We're communicating a level of trust in their abilities. We don't have to be parents 200 percent of the time.

Outside Professionals—New Guides

Sometimes kids need more guidance than a parent can offer; sometimes kids need professional help: learning specialists, therapists, counselors, tutors, and so on. Unfortunately, too often when parents involve some type of professional, they also begin to take over more of the child's domain. In my experience, when children face learning, emotional, or behavioral struggles, parents become even more engaged in the leather-laying process. This of course stems from a natural urge to help and protect, yet it only impedes the child's internal resource development. These kids need moccasins the most. In fact, moccasins enable kids to make more use of what is in their lives—whether it be a teacher, therapist, or coach.

A neighbor of mine happens to be a special education teacher and reading specialist. She revealed: "It was like night and day when I had a student come in to get help who was self-directed and engaged, and another one who wasn't. Some kids knew they needed help with reading—they would come in and sit down, and we would get right to work. Other kids would not even sit at the desk; our whole time together was like a game of negotiation, with the child testing me. I had to focus on basic rules, and so much of our time together was spent on behavioral management that only 5 percent of the time was spent reading."

She told me another revealing story: "I was telling a mother about her son's struggles in math in a parent-teacher conference once, and she instantly replied, 'I'm terrible at math.' But I was referring to her son." She saw how, when parents look at their children through the projected lenses of their own selves, they will never hold their children accountable, nor see their child as a separate individual. This story is actually quite an astute description of parent-child enmeshment. It's unclear who is being discussed—the parent or the child? This enmeshment complicates the process of asking a child to follow through with his own learning and his own education.

Some parents go to dozens and dozens of professionals—to little avail. When a child expects to be rescued, and expects others to move boulders and cushion falls, the best specialists are unable to help. When kids feel that it is up to others to change their lives, they will never reap the benefits of professional help.

Ownership/Accountability

Trying to solve our children's problems is a waste of our energy because these problems fall into our children's domain; hence they are their responsibility, not ours. Master psychotherapist Irvin Yalom writes in *Love's Executioner*, "The first step in all therapeutic change is responsibility assumption. If one feels in no way responsible for one's predicament, then how can one change it?" Many kids today externalize their problems and eschew responsibility for their lives, conveniently handing responsibility over to their parents. This nonassumption of responsibility corresponds with feelings of helplessness, powerlessness, depression, and despair.

Yet this is also an exciting notion, because once kids own their problems, they actually are freed up to change anything and everything—because the power is within them. I frequently use the example of diabetes. If a child has diabetes, at some point he has to assume responsibility for monitoring his sugar intake and insulin levels in order to stay alive. A parent might oversee this for a small child, but it is essential for a school-aged child to begin this process of self-regulation. No one can rescue a child from diabetes; a child must master the art of self-care, because the consequences are great. With ownership and self-care, a child with diabetes can still live a productive life with the ability to pursue her interests and passions.

What if we looked at ADHD, bipolar disorder, or anxiety—at clinical or subclinical levels—the same way as diabetes? With medical management, self-regulation skills, and internal resources these issues do not need to impede one's dreams in life. Unfortunately, since there isn't an immediate threat if they slack off and shirk responsibility for managing their moods, many kids do not take ownership of these issues; they expect others to adapt to them. Many people with mental health or emotional struggles feel like victims and as a result may feel stuck and helpless. But they still have choices.

Temple Grandin

I recently fell in love with the movie *Temple Grandin*, which portrays the life of a woman with autism—it's an inspiring story of a woman who takes responsibility for her life struggle and seemingly achieves the impossible. According to the movie, her mother never tried to make her life easy; she kept holding her daughter to all the same developmental tasks and milestones as her peers. Her mother must have known the goal was not to move her daughter's boulders out of the way; the goal was for Temple to learn to master her own boulder: autism.

Despite the limited knowledge of autism her mother, Eustacia, must have had in 1950 when Temple was diagnosed, she knew her daughter needed to learn the same skills as every other child—it would just be harder. Instead of sending her daughter to an institution (which is what typically happened in the '50s), she kept her on course—learning to talk, mastering rules and manners, completing high school and college, and pursuing her potential. Along the way, Temple learned the necessary coping skills to go from one stage in her life to the next.

In one of the first scenes in the movie, Temple reveals her learned life skill of greeting others. "Hi, I am Temple Grandin. It is nice to meet you." Temple repeated this greeting over and over because it was an essential skill for someone with social anxiety, an inability to read subtleties, and an inability to tolerate loud sounds. It may sound small but this simple social skill of "greeting" others opened doors for her. Many parents may speak for their child with developmental difficulties, but Temple learned to speak for herself.

After high school, Temple went to live on her aunt's cattle farm in California. There she realized that she could relate to and understand cows in a way that "neurotypical" people did not. She noted that distressed cows relaxed when they were squeezed in a metal grate that was used to still cows when they needed to be inoculated. She could see and feel the muscles in the cow relaxing and their bodies becoming quiet. One day shortly thereafter, Temple erupted into one of her tantrums. Yet, even as she ran around screaming, she was also problem-solving; she ran straight to the metal grate and pulled the walls in to squeeze her, just as they'd squeezed the cows. With this, Temple relaxed. She soon devised her own "squeeze machine" to help regulate her emotions. Temple assumed responsibility for her disability, and though it wasn't easy, she worked hard to mitigate her struggles.

As Temple moved through college and the rest of her life, there were many, many bumps along the way, yet she continued to use her intelligence to solve her problems. She began to openly talk about her autism to explain how she saw the world differently to help "neurotypical" people understand her. She got her BS, her MS, and eventually her doctorate. She became an innovator of cattle ranch design and a professor; one could argue she actualized her potential.

In a moving moment at the end of the film, Temple attended one of the first autism conferences. When she stood up and began to speak, the people assumed at first that she was a mother of an autistic child. When Temple corrected them, many in the audience asked how she had become so successful. Temple said, "Well, my mother. She taught me manners and rules and sent me to school even if I didn't want to." Temple is someone with a lifelong disability, yet she navigates life with a sturdy pair of moccasins and is an inspiration.

Asking kids to struggle, to do something hard, even when they themselves have some emotional sensitivity or disability, enables them to keep developing and keep moving forward and maturing in life. It also sends them the message that they are capable, that they can do it. Parents can't skip these steps by trying to take away obstacles, remove struggles, and rescue their kids. Kids need to develop their own internal resources, own their problems, and become invested in their own lives. Temple is a real example of someone who has done this.

In his autobiography *Novice to Master*, Soko Morinaga Roshi tells a story of a monk named Ken who was sent on a long journey by his master:

> The younger monk suddenly broke into tears. "I have been practicing for many years, and I still haven't been able to attain anything. Now, here I am roaming around the country on this trip; there's no way I am going to attain enlightenment this way," Ken lamented.
>
> When he heard this, Genjoza, thrusting all his strength into his words, put himself at the junior monk's disposal: "I will take care of anything that I can take care of for you on this trip," he said. "But there are just five things that I cannot do in your place. I can't wear clothes for you. I can't eat for you. I can't shit for you. I can't piss for you. And I can't carry your body around and live your life for you."
>
> It is said that upon hearing these words, the monk Ken suddenly awakened from his deluded dream and attained a great enlightenment.

When we leave our child's boulder on his trail, we let the problem stay in his lap—we make our children responsible and trust their intelligence and natural ability to problem-solve. We are removing the leather and asking them to make their own moccasins, their own protection.

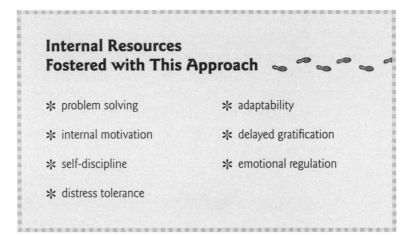

**Internal Resources
Fostered with This Approach**

* problem solving   * adaptability

* internal motivation   * delayed gratification

* self-discipline   * emotional regulation

* distress tolerance

CHAPTER 9

Skill: Sorting Out the Boulders

....

Trying to smooth everything out to avoid confrontation, not to rock the boat,
is not what's meant by compassion or patience. It's what is meant by control.
Then you are not trying to step into unknown territory, to find yourself more
naked with less protection and therefore more in contact with reality.

—**Pema Chodron,** *Start Where You Are*

....

Isabel and Julia

Sixteen-year-old Isabel texted her mother, Julia, almost hourly from high
school. They were friends on Facebook. They shopped together, gossiped
about celebrities together, and watched shows together. Julia said that
when Isabel was growing up she always wanted to be with her, even if
they were just doing errands together. Although she disliked the term,
Isabel was her mother's "best friend," in the sense that she was the one
she talked to the most. Julia, though somewhat hesitant to admit it, felt
rewarded in her relationship with her daughter and even felt a bit smug
when she heard about the stress in other mother-daughter relationships.

Owen, Julia's husband, was equally smitten with his daughter and
delighted in the closeness they had as a family. He remarked, "I don't
know what we're going to do when she goes to college. Who will we
talk to every day? Even Isabel said at her doctor's appointment yesterday
that she will never go to a checkup without her mother; she only feels
comfortable when her mother is there. It's so hard to invest so much in a
child whom we love so much, who brings so much joy, who is such a part
of our lives, who will one day walk out and leave us."

Two years later, this family was driving their daughter to college, settling her into her new dorm room, unpacking her freshly bought college

clothes, and staring into a new vacuum. Then, without any predeparture discussions, this family set up a new routine eerily similar to the old. They were still in touch with their daughter—not just once a day, but multiple times a day. Dad called in the morning on his way to work to wake her up, check on her schedule for the day, and ask if she had finished her homework assignments (he had a copy of her class schedule and course syllabuses). Mom was in touch throughout the day—texting hello, calling, even Facebooking her daughter's new friends. They emailed over her coursework; her parents edited her papers, as they had done since elementary school. Finally Isabel and her mom caught up on the phone at night to hear about her day, her friends, parties, and any other details. Mom and Dad were soon looking into real estate in the college area; it was in a beautiful country setting, and it would be easy for Isabel to come and relax with her friends on the weekend.

Occasionally Isabel would complain, "They know I'm in class; why are they texting me?" But she still reinforced this relationship pattern by reaching out to them with the same frequency.

Yet when Julia and Owen came up to take her out to dinner, they could tell something was askew with Isabel. She was sullen. She had lost a bit of her sparkle. She seemed fragile and on edge. Isabel admitted to struggling with the academic workload. It was also clear that she had not really made friends or even connected much with her roommate—since Isabel was always on the phone with her parents or her high school buds. Isabel wondered if she knew how to make new friends. She missed home, she said, and right there in the middle of the restaurant she placed her head in her folded arms and cried. Sobbed. She begged: Could she please come home? She even presented a plan to live at home and attend a local college.

Her parents were aghast. And for once in their lives they were at a loss for words. Should they let her come home? They missed her. Should they tell her she would be fine? They were not sure that would be true. They hated to see her sad; they were completely overwhelmed. How could they fix this?

After Julia and Owen stayed an extra day and had Isabel spend a night in their hotel, they were able to temporarily ward off decision making by asking Isabel to finish the first quarter. They promised that when she came home for fall break they would have a thorough discussion about college. Julia, for the first time ever, had grave concerns about her daughter and, moreover, about their mother-daughter relationship. She began to wonder if they were "too close." She felt paralyzed.

Julia reflected on past conflicts she'd had with Isabel. Occasionally when something was wrong, Isabel would "sass" her, with a snap in her tone, and Julia would usually react defensively but then swiftly try to comfort her. This usually led to a quick reconciliation, as both were uncomfortable with conflict. But now Julia was presented with an unavoidable conflict. Of course she wanted her daughter home, of course she missed her, but she did not want her to go to a local community college. That was not the plan. She quickly found a therapist to help her get some insight and perspective since she knew she was not alone; many families have rocky college transitions.

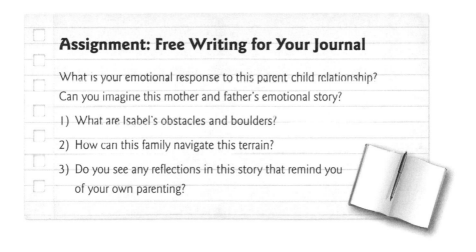

Assignment: Free Writing for Your Journal

What is your emotional response to this parent child relationship?
Can you imagine this mother and father's emotional story?

1) What are Isabel's obstacles and boulders?

2) How can this family navigate this terrain?

3) Do you see any reflections in this story that remind you of your own parenting?

William and Chuck

An important skill that many families need to learn is how to sort out which feelings, thoughts, and behaviors belong to which member of the family. When parents take on their children's problems, and when children take on parents' problems, everyone gets stuck. Sorting out can only happen through ownership and accountability. When parents own their part, their feeling, their fear, then the child can identify what is hers. What makes this so effective is that it sidesteps blame and power struggles and allows family members to become self-aware and accountable. This process is a useful and safe way to work through conflict and allow the family to move forward in a healthy direction. It is similar to the concept introduced in a previous chapter—cleaning up your own side of the street.

Twelve-year-old William and his dad had a day out together, biking to the pool for a swim. Chuck, grateful for a day off from his demanding job, was thrilled to be with his boy. They hopped on their bikes, but immediately William was doing a lot of showing off: looking for jumps, speeding up and skidding his tires, and taking his hands off the bars and making funny faces. Chuck felt heat building around his neck and face and prompted William to settle down, though he want to avoid a conflict. William, however, thought he was being funny; his dad was usually into roughing around.

William raced his dad around corners and then when the pool was in sight he took off. Chuck found himself getting more annoyed. As they locked their bikes up, Chuck reminded him once again to settle down. Hot from the ride, they both jumped into the pool to cool off.

William, feeling a bit jittery and awkward since he was not with his dad that much, began splashing around in the pool. He kept splashing his dad in the face and laughing. Chuck asked him to stop and then stop again, but William kept splashing. Chuck finally erupted into anger and screamed at William: "Stop it right now! We're out of here." William ran out of the pool crying and called his mother and said he never wanted to do stuff with dad again.

In processing this event in therapy we tried to sort out what happened. Chuck was able to identify that he knows William is impulsive and at times erratic; that's William's pattern. Yet when William splashed him, he took it personally. He admitted, "That's one of my problems; I assume when people do things to me it's on purpose, and personal, and so it triggers me." Chuck also admitted to being really excited about spending time with William and being annoyed when he realized the outing was not going well. He felt William was "pushing his buttons." When asked to own what was his, Chuck admitted that he had expectations for the outing. He was taking William's behavior personally, and he avoided having any conflict until it was too late and he blew up.

William said he was just trying to have fun and laugh. Then he hung his head and said he was sorry and that he should have stopped. He said sometimes he's not comfortable around his dad.

In this scenario, the family is actually making huge progress in communication because each is identifying his own part—they are both stepping away from blame and are sharing their own experience. Dad asserted, "I will work on giving you feedback, setting limits, and not taking your behavior personally. If you are upset with me about something, I hope you can let me know." William replied, "Thanks Dad, I'll try to listen better when you ask me to stop."

Skill: Let's try to apply the parenting techniques described in this book to this scenario. What could Dad do differently?

1) When William was biking in a reckless manner, Chuck could have asked him to stop and attuned to him right away. "Hey bud, I notice you're going a bit crazy on the bike. Can you tell me what is going on?"

2) Chuck could set a limit. "Okay, William, I want you to know that we can head home and drive to the pool. If your biking gets reckless again, we'll just have to go back. Okay?"

3) Dad could attune in another way: "Hey, I like playing around too, but it doesn't feel safe on this sidewalk, near cars, roads, and people's driveways. If you want we can go out to the dirt bike area and play around another time."

A twelve-year-old boy may not know exactly what he is feeling or know why he is so restless and jittery. Parents can't change this, nor can they change kid's internal states, but they can attune to their children and try to contain them by setting limits. When parents attune and mirror back what they see, kids usually feel seen and heard on some level, which helps them learn to shift and self-regulate.

Isabel and Julia

Let's apply these same concepts of sorting out the boulders to the mother-daughter scenario discussed earlier. Julia, the mother, has developed some new self-awareness from working with a therapist. She could start by using the I-feel format:

~~~~~~

Julia: "You know, Isabel, I felt sad and upset and worried when I heard that you wanted to come home from college. I feel this way because I think you may be too dependent on us, and I am probably too dependent on you. It's not fair for you to come home and take care of us, nor do we need to keep taking care of you. We started college off on the wrong foot—talking too much each day. We love you so much, but we don't want to prevent you from living your life and pursuing your dreams. I think I call too much; maybe we're too close."

Isabel: "Well, I want you to call, Mom—you help me get through things."

Julia: "Well, we can still talk, but how about once a day?"

isabel: "That's going to be hard. I feel angry that I can't just come home."

Julia: "Well, thank you for telling me how you feel. I'm okay with your anger. It's justified; I've been too dependent on you. But I want you to try college again. I know you and trust you, and we believe that you can do it. It's not easy for kids to go off to college, but I also know that you're really intelligent and creative. Do you see any ways to problem-solve your dilemma?"

Isabel: "I'll think about it."

Julia: "Okay. We're going to be fine; I'm looking at some new jobs and Dad is getting into tennis. We'll work on figuring it out on our end, and we'll let you be in charge of how you want to solve it on your end."

Isabel: "Thanks Mom."

Julia: "Is there anything else you want to talk about?"

Isabel: "I'm not sure, but I think I *will* have more time to focus on school if we only connect once a day. I actually really like my English class, but a lot of the time I feel lonely and sad—which I never felt at home."

Julia: "I feel lonely and sad sometimes too; they're normal feelings and part of change. You're growing up."

Isabel: "I know."

Julia: "Also, I'm going to ask that you go to the academic center to get help with editing your papers. Dad and I would love to read what you write, but only after you've had some chance to get help at the college. We can't be your editors anymore."

Isabel: "That's really annoying, Mom."

Julia: "I know."

~~~~~~

In this exchange, Julia took ownership for her feelings, her dependency, and her overinvolvement with her daughter. She also set some boundaries: go back to college, one contact a day, use the academic center. She let the problem of college stay in her daughter's lap. She did not try to "fix" the situation or make it easier for her daughter, instead she validated that it's okay if it's hard and encouraged Isabel to problem-solve. Julia did not rescue her.

Isabel, though not as aware of her role, did admit to feelings of loneliness and sadness that she never felt at home. But mostly she seemed confused. Since she was not sure about what she wanted, she seemed willing to give college another try.

Parents need to give their children space so they can undergo the natural separation and individuation process that is part of identity development. Kids become clearer with their identities when parents allow them to wrestle with their own problems. Adversity is part of every person's life and exists for a reason; kids build esteem and confidence when they problem-solve on their own.

It should be noted that both vignettes in this chapter had positive outcomes because the parents took the initiative when it came to claiming responsibility. As parents we are frequently spotlighting our children's behaviors, yet when we model accountability and own our boulders, chances are our children will feel less shamed and more willing to see their part in conflicts. Taking responsibility is part of maturing and moccasin making. It's much easier to highlight another's problems, yet when we don't acknowledge our part it's unlikely that kids will take genuine responsibility for theirs.

Remember—the only thing we can control is the fertile soil of the home, where we can model healthy habits such as taking responsibility. We can't control what is out in the world, off the edge of the leather. We can't make our kids be emotionally mature and self-aware—but we can demonstrate such qualities.

Of course, as a parent myself, I have to work on all these concepts all the time because my children hand me daily opportunities to practice. The other day, for instance, when I picked my daughter up from preschool I hadn't packed her lunch, as I do sometimes, because we were going to go home for lunch instead. Feeling tired and hungry already, she wailed. I then told her that I needed to do a quick errand on the way home, since that was the only time that day I could attend to it, which would add about ten more minutes to the drive home. Well, as you can imagine, she continued to scream, with what seemed like pure full-bodied emotion. A variety of thoughts and feelings passed through me: tension and annoyance from her screaming, sadness that she was hungry, anxiety to fix her crying and to get home.

I then reminded myself that she's still four and that it's normal for her to feel strong emotions, especially when not getting her way. She's allowed to feel sad, so I'll let her cry as much as she wants. I made a few comments such as "I hear how upset and disappointed you are." I was tempted to blow off my errand but knew that still might not make her happy, and it really was something I needed to get done that day. She then began to yell at me. I felt the urge to yell back because of the way she was carrying on, but I paused and gently said, "You're allowed to feel sad, honey, but you're not allowed to yell at me." She stopped yelling. After I did my quick errand and got back in the car, she was quiet. I asked her a few questions about her day, and I shared a quick story about my day. She then began humming and playing with some stickers. By the time we got home, she had forgotten all about her disappointment and wanted to make her lunch with me. I did not touch her boulder of sadness and disappointment; I acknowledged it, and she navigated it.

PART IV

Two Trails Side by Side

CHAPTER 10

New Pathways

....

*A true teacher wants nothing more than to see you stand
on your own two feet.*
—Ezra Bayda with Josh Bartok, *Saying Yes to Life (Even the Hard Parts)*

....

Often parents fear that if they refrain from rescuing their child they will lose their parent-child connection. Although parents may understand their worrying and hovering is problematic, at least it's a comfortable, familiar, and reliable way to relate to their child. Examining and changing these patterns *is* scary. Parents wonder what they *are* supposed to do—not care? Shouldn't parents help and fix? For many, this touches on very primal instincts, on what it means to raise children, on what it means to be a parent.

This notion actually goes even deeper than parenting. Refraining from helping and fixing can provoke a fundamental feeling of aloneness, even an existential anxiety. When we take our children away, we are left with ourselves. Many of us like to keep busy and distracted with our children's problems or simply organizing and managing their lives. We feel a sense of purpose in these activities. We want to feel useful. So we keep plodding along, steering and directing, in an attempt to keep the lurking anxiety in the background. There are many words for this anxiety: emptiness, the void, Buddhism names it *dukkha*, existential psychotherapist Irvin Yalom calls it "existence pain."

Existence pain relates to purpose and meaning—that is, to the fear of not having purpose and meaning, to knowing our lives are ultimately finite. Much of Western culture is about filling that pain with stuff, escaping the void with medication or other substances, distracting ourselves from the emptiness with endless screens and gadgets, or fighting the duk-kha through achievement and accumulation. Some go to therapy to get to the root of their pain, to try to unearth some memory or insight about their childhood. Some dedicate themselves to religion. We all do what-ever we can to eradicate this existence pain, or to at least keep busy and buzzing along on the surface enough to not notice it so much.

Understandably, then, we're quick to shield our children from any exis-tence pain. However, they too have entered the world in a finite body and will also experience human emotions, physical and emotional pain, illness, and at some point death. Can we instead acknowledge, validate, and normalize these feelings instead of the constant safeguarding and hypervigilance against them?

The teachings of Buddhism reveal that the problem is actually the effort to remove emptiness, not the emptiness itself. Psychiatrist and Buddhist Mark Epstein writes in *Going to Pieces Without Falling Apart* that thera-pists have always been "trying to get rid of emptiness by uncovering its cause. From Freud and his followers on down, therapists had identified all kinds of plausible causes. Buddhism, as I was learning, sought to turn the Western experience of emptiness around. The problem with the Western experience of emptiness was that it was mixed with so much fear." The word *emptiness* does not carry a negative tone or feeling in Buddhism; the way I understand Buddhist emptiness is simply as the opposite of solid. A piece of wood, for instance, can be solid or it can be hollow—and thus, empty. Things are not as solid as we think.

For example, at times we may think, "I am never going to get it right" or "I am a terrible person" or "My child is so frustrating." Yet these are just thoughts, which are not very solid; they are transient and they could change in the course of twenty minutes. So in Buddhist terms we could say these thoughts are empty, just as ideas or perspectives are empty, in the sense that they too can change and shift.

I once spoke to a man at a Buddhist center in Vermont who had com-pleted a one-month-long retreat of silence and meditation, during which the participants were only allowed to have "functional speech." He shared how after a week or so of not talking to the fellow participants, he started to make up all sorts of stories and projections in his mind. He identified who he would be friends with, who he liked and did not like, who was good and who was bad—all sorts of labels. He even began to make up life stories for the other people also on retreat. With lots of reflection time he began to see how silly his thoughts were—he hadn't actually ever had a conversation with any of these people he was analyzing. Yet that is what our minds do: categorize, sort, label, and judge. He discovered firsthand that his thoughts were not very solid or reliable. And, of course, he came to understand his peers quite differently once he was able to meet them and get to know them.

Buddhists practice nonattachment to these impermanent thoughts and feelings, so what is left is just presence—just being. Buddhism works to break down the nonsolid boxes and labels in the thinking mind to simply experience the present moment. Thus, "emptiness" could also be called *openness* or even *freedom*. Emptiness is not something to be afraid of; in fact, as Mark Epstein writes, it's "an understanding of one's true nature, an intuition of the absence of inherent identity in people or in things."

What would happen if we allowed ourselves to be with our own feelings of emptiness, rather than constantly trying to fill or fix these feelings in our children and in ourselves? We would at least view our children's pain differently and would perhaps open up to a feeling of intimacy and sharing with our children.

What I am suggesting is not "detaching" from your children, nor am I suggesting that you ignore their struggle and concerns. Instead, empathize with your child in a new way. When parents relate to their children with an awareness of their own feelings, chances are they are more likely to be present and accepting of their child's feelings.

Sharing Instead of Fixing: Trail Guiding

If parents are ready to relinquish their roles as trail managers, or at least ready to experiment with a new way of parenting, I present the idea of *trail guiding*. Instead of moving all the boulders out of the way and laying down leather all over the ground, parents can guide from a trail right next to the child. Parents are present, attentive, yet respectful of their child's boundaries. Kids are more willing to share their inner worlds when there is adequate freedom and space within their own boundaries, when they feel they have something that is their own.

The following diagrams portray these two different styles:

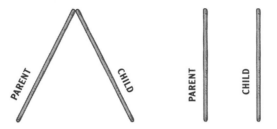

	Diagram 1	Diagram 2
Parent Role	Trail Manager	Trail Guide
Relationship	Unstable	Stable
Boundaries	Enmeshed	Clear

Although diagram 1 may appear stable, it can easily become unstable when a child or parent pulls away in conflict. In this arrangement, the parent has to go into the child's domain, and as a result the child expects the parent to be there to fix, solve, and rescue. Yet this arrangement also fosters feelings of dependency and helplessness in the child, which spurs a variety of ways of acting out.

In diagram 2 the parent and child are stable and side by side. The parent isn't going anywhere—he or she is present and attentive but respects the child's domain. The parent allows the child to feel, struggle, and share; he or she can pull away and then come back. The parent stays present and close, but does not encroach into the child's territory. The parent accepts all of the child's feelings and sets limits on behaviors that are inappropriate.

In diagram 1, the parent is managing the child and taking responsibility for the child's problems and struggles. In diagram 2 the parent, as guide, is accountable for his or her own thoughts, feelings, and actions;

in return, the child takes responsibility for the child's thoughts, feelings, and behaviors. This creates stability and closeness and fosters maturation and individuation.

In diagram 2, the parent may feel more aloneness, more existence pain. Yet this parent may also feel more feelings of freedom and independence. The same is also true for the child—there may be more aloneness, freedom, and independence. This sense of a separate self can be mirrored and framed positively. In the arrangement in diagram 2, there is a healthy space for two separate individuals side by side, where sharing thoughts and feelings is the emotional glue in the parent-child relationship.

Trail Guiding

Mother: "How does your day look today?" *How does your trail look today?*

Son: "Well, I'm worried about my presentation in history and also about seeing Karen because we got in a fight yesterday." *Mom, there's a huge boulder on the left and some sharp rocks around it.*

Mother, validating the obstacle: "That sounds difficult, what do you think you will do?" *That sounds challenging, what looks like the best way around from your perspective?*

Son: "I've prepped a ton for the presentation, so at this point, whatever, I guess I'll see what happens. With Karen it's harder, but I guess I'll just ask her if she wants to talk about it." *Well I think it might be best to climb over the boulder to avoid the sharp rocks. I'll just have to be careful coming down.*

Mother: "Okay, tell me how it goes." *Okay, let me know how it looks after you're over it.*

Son, later in the day: "Hey Mom. I messed up in the beginning of the presentation and had to start over. It was embarrassing, but that was the hardest part; once I started going it actually went well. And Karen and I talked so I feel better, but I'm not sure what's going to happen." *I got down, Mom. I scrapped my knee, but it's okay. Now the*

trail looks pretty smooth, though I can't see too far ahead. I think it'll
be okay. I'll let you know.

Mother: "I'm glad the presentation went well. I imagine that's hard
with Karen since you two have been together for a while—I'm here
if you want to talk more." *I'm glad to hear you're okay. I'll still be*
on my parallel trail if you need any more guidance.

~~~~~~

Present but Not Interfering:
Giving Children the Capacity to Be

Children want to solve their own problems, and moreover, they want
to *share*. When kids share they are letting their parents into their inner
worlds. They're letting their parents know their problems, how they solve
them, how they think, and how they feel. This is emotional intimacy. Parents can have emotional closeness and emotional intimacy without fixing
or rescuing. In fact the aloneness a child feels within the proper boundaries of a parent-child relationship is critical for healthy child development.

Epstein writes that parents must be "present but not interfering," which
"creates a holding environment that nourishes the child." Creating the
space for a child to be alone is just as important as meeting our children's
physical needs. When parents strike the balance between not intruding
and not abandoning, kids are free to explore their selves. Epstein refers to
this space as "the capacity to be." Guiding your children from a parallel
trail allows them to be within their own space and boundaries.

Intrusive parents foster more closed children. It is always striking to
me to learn how little overinvolved parents know of their child's inner
world. These parents work so hard to direct and manage all the details of
their child's life, yet they know the least. Kids who are enmeshed don't tell
their parents their innermost thoughts and feelings; they only tell their
parents what they need or want: a ride to the mall, new jeans, pizza for
dinner, and so on. With a lack of sharing in the parent-child relationship,
parents instead work even harder to read their children's cues by guess-
ing their emotions, which just causes the child to build more barriers.
The problem with this pattern is children aren't learning to open up,

be vulnerable, and share—which is part of emotional maturation and emotional intimacy.

But even more problematic is that many parents guess, assume, and decode incorrectly and miss what's really going on. Parents aren't mind readers. Just like the man I met on retreat, we often make up stories and assumptions that are wrong. When parents wrongly assume a child is upset about one thing and try to fix it, they miss where their child really is. This can provoke more acting out, resistance, or shutting down from the child.

What children want most is to be known and accepted. Parents need to ask, not assume. Parents need to elicit the child's thoughts and feelings; when a child is closed off, a parent can mirror and attune. For example, rather than making assumptions, a parent can ask, "Sweetie, I see that you went to your room after school. You look upset. Can you tell me what you're feeling?" If the child refuses to answer, the parent can just respond, "Well, I don't want to guess and get it wrong, but I'm here if you want to share or let me know if you are upset about something." This parent is present and receptive, but respects the child's domain. This parent is not filling in the gaps. Children often say, "You just don't understand." And rather than getting defensive we can say, "You're right, I can't read your mind, but I would love to listen if you want to share." We have to leave that space for children to decide to participate in the family.

Exciting research shows that experimenting with new behaviors and experiencing new behavioral and emotional outcomes can actually form new pathways in the brain. This is called *neuroplasticity* and indicates that the brain is malleable rather than fixed—empty, not solid. Although changing behaviors and automatic responses is not easy, it is possible. As parents reinforce these new responses, such as reflective listening, attunement, validating, pausing, reframing, and setting necessary limits, they are strengthening this new response system.

But to make these neurological changes, parents have to be willing to take risks, to leave old patterns and experiment with new responses. Refraining from old ways, though, is extremely hard to do and can even provoke feelings of loneliness, powerlessness, or lack of purpose. It's normal to feel scared when exploring new territory. Yet parents must remember that when they open up to fear, the unknown, or even existence pain, they are alive and present in their bodies—this is a good thing. This is exactly the process of moccasin building. This is what we want to be modeling to our children.

In the parent-child relationship, trail guiding, as opposed to trail managing, means listening, staying present, and pausing from action. You are accepting whatever feeling or struggle your child is having. Parents need to show their children that they can handle it—they don't need to be protected from the child's reality. Children want to share and are more likely to share when they know you're not going to take over their trail: that is, either abandon them or interfere with their path. Instead, there is mutual respect. Trail guiding, in fact, creates stability and promotes maturation, resilience, and interdependence.

When we're brave enough to be alone in our own pain, we'll be more likely to foster that space for our children. This doesn't have to be scary; every separate individual person on the planet experiences dukkha. Instead we can share this journey with our children and validate that pain, loneliness, and uncertainty are normal feelings. Trail guiding can allow families to share feelings of emotional closeness—not just the physical proximity of living under the same roof.

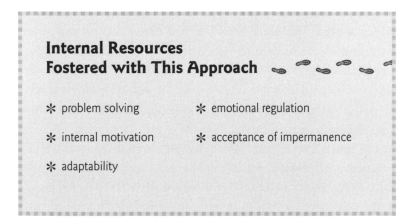

Internal Resources
Fostered with This Approach

* problem solving

* internal motivation

* adaptability

* emotional regulation

* acceptance of impermanence

CHAPTER 11

Compassion

Compassion is the best healer.
—**Lama Zopa Rinpoche,** *Ultimate Healing*

Emotions are a normal part of the human experience—they are neither good nor bad. Just like an orchid flower blooms, wilts, falls off, rebuds, and blooms again, our feelings cycle through us. When we intervene in our children's emotional process we are interfering with this cycle. The same is true for struggle; when we intervene in our child's struggle, we are disrupting our child's natural ability to problem-solve, to grow and mature. Sometimes these concepts, however, are not so easy to apply to our children, but what is needed instead of action is compassion.

Tibetan Buddhist teacher Pema Chodron's definition of compassion is a telling one: compassion is what a mother with no arms feels when her child falls in the river. I've spent some time with this one. At first I tossed it out of my consciousness because it seemed too hard to relate to, but it found a way back into my thoughts in my work with parents. Parents come to me with many painful scenarios—a child who has given up on school or won't get out of bed, who lies incessantly, or who spends hours engaged in anxiety rituals or computer addictions—and the parents have generally spent endless hours fixing, nudging, or cajoling their child. Most parents have done everything they could, to no avail. We're more comfortable with action than with feeling.

A mother with no arms: a feeling of helplessness. We often feel helpless when it comes to our children's pain. Yet there is value in staying right there with your child and feeling the reservoir of compassion that we all have for our children, just like the mother by the river. This mother can't fix her child's problem, but she can feel. That is compassion. Compassion means we are aware of our own suffering, so we can relate—or try to relate—to another's suffering. Most of us know physical pain, emotional pain; we know how rejection feels, we know fear, and we know loss, anxiety, and despair. We can feel with them. There is an internal softening, a sense of "this is hard, this is painful, and *I am right here with you.*" But we can't reach in and remove another person's suffering, just as this mother can't scoop her child up out of the river.

The Dalai Lama's take on compassion is profound. He writes in *An Open Heart,* "When our focus is on others, on our wish to free them from their misery—this is compassion. However, only once we have acknowledged our own state of suffering and developed the wish to free ourselves from it can we have a truly meaningful wish to free others from their misery." In this sense, compassion is not "fixing" the other but is remaining deeply rooted in the human experience while staying present with another. It is as if a parent is sharing a child's pain rather than fixing a pain. Instead of identifying something that is "wrong" in a child, there is a sense of normalizing pain as part of the human experience—no matter how great the pain or its cause, even if it's adoption pain, autism, or sexual identity confusion. Although a parent may be heterosexual or may not be adopted or may not have autism, and thus may not understand the uniqueness of those feelings, a parent can still have compassion by working on freeing his or her own suffering.

We cannot give up our own growth for the cause of another who appears to be in more pain. In fact the way we help others is to be aware of and in touch with our own pain. Sometimes a struggling child can help us touch into this notion.

Jack

Jack, an exuberant ten-year-old, began fixating on decisions shortly after he turned ten. He could not decide which jacket, or shirt, or shoes to wear to school. His inability to make decisions led to a feeling of paralysis. Eventually, he began giving up on schoolwork and then refused to go to school altogether. His parents, baffled with the situation, cycled through a series of responses. First they went into his room and told him they didn't care what he wore—whether it was shorts on a cool day or boots on a warm day. Then they went in and picked out what he should wear, attempting to eliminate his indecision. Finally they yelled, they cajoled, they bargained. At last, exasperated, they gave up, feeling defeated.

Jack harbored a feeling that something was wrong with him. Everyone else seemed "fine" and did not worry about school or clothes. Jack was struggling with insecurity and sexual orientation issues that he did not understand, and he was incredibly anxious. On some level, his parents viewed Jack's anxiety and paralysis as some type of failure on their part. They must have caused it, or they simply must work harder to fix it. Rather than empathize with his human emotions, they wanted to fix his struggles and when they were unable they blamed their child and then blamed themselves.

Buddhist and clinical psychologist Tara Brach reveals in *Radical Acceptance* that a core misconception that many of us carry is that something is wrong with us if we experience a negative emotion. I think we can all agree that something is wrong when a child refuses school and stays in bed, yet there is nothing wrong with feeling anxious, worried, or confused. In fact these are feelings we all feel every day. Jack simply did not know how to navigate his anxiety. This is an area where parents can try to turn the tide when they see their children struggling, acting out, or shutting down. Parents can listen, attune, stay present, validate, normalize, and show compassion. Even if the child does not know what is wrong.

Recently my youngest daughter started to randomly tell me, "Mom, I'm worrying." I would say, "What are you worried about?" With tension in her voice she would say, "I don't know! I'm just worried." I felt a strong urge to jump in and fix it and say, "Everything is okay," or "Don't worry," or try to cheer her up. But instead I began to say, "It's okay to be worried, sweetie." She would sit with it for a bit. Then I would say, "Thanks for sharing your feeling; I'm here to listen."

This went on for a month or so—every few days she would remind me that she was worried again. I followed with the same response: "It's okay to be worried." I would also add, "I get worried too—it's a normal feeling." Or, rather than actually doing something to fix it, I would ask, "Is there anything I can do?" She would politely reply, "No thanks, Mom." I let her stay in charge of the feeling. We all have worries, they're nothing to get alarmed about, and it's best to learn to process worry naturally. Of course I don't know for certain, but it occurred to me that she might be feeling an existential worry about the uncertainty of life or maybe she had begun to ponder death, since she did not relate her worry to anything specific. These unidentified worries are sometimes the hardest because our thinking minds want to solve them and are unable.

Her feeling of worry and the tension in her voice continued on and off for a few more weeks. Until one day in the car, I noticed a significant shift. My daughter said confidently, "I'm worried again, but I know it's okay." Her tone was calm and there was no tension or fear in her voice. She was aware of her feeling but not reacting to it. I noticed that my responses of validation and normalizing had helped; she was able to move on. I still don't know what her worry was about, but the goal isn't to remove negative emotions by fixing—it's to validate and normalize feelings, which allows them to pass through their cycle. Compassion, as described in Buddhist tradition, means acknowledging and accepting what is there.

When Do We Act?

In *Be Beautiful, Be Yourself*, Vietnamese Zen Buddhist monk Thich Nhat Hanh suggests the following: "When you feel overwhelmed, you're trying too hard. That kind of energy does not help the other person, and it does not help you. You should not be too eager to help right away. There are two things: to be and to do. Don't think too much about to do—to be is first."

The urge to fix, help, and solve for children is of course universal. Our emotions are deeply intertwined with our children and most parents simply wish for their children to be happy, so any unhappiness tends to prompt parents into action. Yet it is important to discern when we are actually doing something useful, as opposed to interfering with our children's domain, taking over their problems and discomforts, and disrupting their natural ability to feel and process emotions.

Luckily there is much that is still in our domain that we can do. We can feed our children when they are hungry. We can make them a special snack. We can get them ready for bed when they are tired. We can listen.

We can play games, sing songs, do crafts, play sports, tickle them, and read stories or watch movies together. We can clothe them. We can take them to activities. We can celebrate holidays. We can be attentive to them when they are sick. We can talk about things they don't understand. We can try to answer their questions. We can go on outings together. We can share life with them. So when *do* parents give advice?

Parents should give advice only when it is solicited. When children genuinely ask "Mom, what do you think?" or "Dad, what would you do?" they want another perspective, and parents can freely give their parental advice. But my one caveat is that a parent should still say, "Well, I'll share my perspective, but it is your decision." Remember that parents make a lot of decisions about their children anyway, like whose car they are allowed to get into when their friends start to drive, or what their curfew is, or how much allowance they get, and so on. But if the issue lies in the child's domain, the decision should be made by the child.

So where does comforting come in? Making favorite meals, drawing a bath, watching a movie together, taking a hike, showing affection, going shopping these are all ways to comfort and show love to our children, though we must not think these soothe every ailment. When we realize where our domain ends and our child's begins, this is where the compassion comes in. We can't cross over into their domain. We can't take on their sadness, worry, or hurt feelings like a project. Just like the armless mother can't scoop her child out of the river.

My sense is that all parents have had the experience of when overinvestment in their children's happiness backfires. For example, when we attempt to create the perfect environment for happiness—an ice-cream party, a special cookie at the bakery, a visit to the toy store, or handing a teen our credit card—and these efforts still come up short, and our child is still upset about something. Our children have their own experience of the world—as much as we try, we cannot control what they feel.

This desire to comfort is heightened when a child struggles emotionally. Say your daughter has depression, or academic or social struggles. Parents want to cast that rescue line out and pull their child to safety. But this can be complicated when the child is acting out. When the parents are dealing with varying degrees of inappropriate behaviors, it's hard for them to see how to be compassionate. Is compassion giving children what they want? Letting them be on the computer all night? Changing the rules or expectations, completing your child's homework, allowing your child's moods to dominate the home—are these ways to show compassion?

It *is* compassionate to establish boundaries and consequences to keep a child on course. Allowing a child to harm himself through giving up on school, staying in bed, and avoiding life, or allowing him to harm others through an anger outburst or emotional manipulation is not compassion. These behaviors do not help a child. Parents can set limits with consequences when dealing with inappropriate conduct—these limits help light a fire underneath stagnant and stuck behaviors. Attunement, compassion, and boundaries—these are the best ways to act compassionately.

Reframing

When we incrementally step away from managing our children's lives and slowly peel back the leather we'd laid on their worlds, we are still actively parenting. Some parents feel they are neglecting their duties when they see all the tasks their child has to do and they sit on their hands instead of helping. But this is not neglect—this is intentional, brave parenting. Parents can simply be present. Thich Nhat Hanh says, "It is like if the other person is sitting at the foot of a tree. The tree does not do anything, but the tree is fresh and alive. When you are like that tree, sending out waves of freshness, you help to calm down the suffering in the other person." We need to own our urges to fix and then practice restraint—we need to "tie ourselves to the mast."

I have urges to rescue my children all the time. Just the other day, my older daughter was disrespectful to me when getting ready for school; she yelled, she sulked, she stalled, and we were late. I told her that it was not okay to yell or make us late for school. I told her that when we got home she would have to spend twenty minutes in her room before she played in the house or with her sister. I told her that I felt sad that we struggled and that I loved her.

I notice that when I do set a boundary it allows my children to stop, shift emotionally, and process their feelings much quicker. Without limits, kids frequently do not know how to stop themselves and self-regulate on their own. Up through adolescence, the brain's prefrontal cortex is still developing, which affects processes such as judgment and impulse control. We can't get mad at our children for not knowing how to self-regulate—we have to compassionately teach them through setting limits. Many parents avoid setting limits and as a result many kids feel out of control. This does not aid in the self-esteem department; if anything, kids feel ashamed when they feel out of control.

After setting the boundary and consequence, my daughter was a delight. She kissed me goodbye at school and when I picked her up from the bus. When we got home, I reminded her of the twenty minutes. She ran to her room. Yet I found myself wanting to shave off the time. I began to think, well, I'll let her out after fifteen minutes. Then I whittled it away to ten. I realized I was feeling guilty. I wanted to rescue her from my consequence. But I also realized that my daughter seemed to be fine, busy playing away in her room. I soon got distracted with her younger sister and before I knew it twenty-five minutes had passed. When I went into her room, she had started a new project and wanted to finish. I realized my urge to rescue her was about me, not her—she knew she was out of line in the morning; she had accepted the consequence and moved on. I was the one feeling guilty about giving her a consequence. And when I stick to consequences, they work.

When we step out of our children's way and refrain, kids will learn lessons and process feelings more naturally. Sometimes when I try to excite my children about something new I bought or some new information about a trip or a holiday, I become disappointed when they don't respond the way I hoped. In short, I am trying to control their feelings. This is so deeply programmed into us parents that it takes laser-like self-awareness to see when we reach to fix and comfort.

The importance of refraining also applies to when we imagine our children will be unhappy or bored, and we try to avoid these moments by entertaining them instead, which of course our culture feeds into with endless gadgets. We may, however, miss an opportunity for our children to be creative and inventive by making use of seemingly unstructured time. I like unstructured time in the mornings or after school, but I struggle with it on the weekends, assuming my children will go crazy without activities (which does happen sometimes). One weekend I returned from doing errands to find my husband working on a project and the kids deep into their imagined play—even after a few hours had passed. They cycled though playing hotel, to school, to delivering mail (creating mailboxes for each of their rooms), and finally playing dance class. If I'd been home, I might have intervened and even prevented this type of play to happen. They barely noticed my return home because they were too busy.

Kids' emotions come and go whether we are trying to make them happy or not. Refraining and pausing is something I need to practice frequently as a mother, because it is so easy to take over and clean their room, fix their problem, or do the chore myself. But what I have learned as a mother and therapist is that "easy" often equals laying down the leather, while "hard" leads to more moccasin building. I have to let my five-year-old make her own peanut-butter-and-jelly sandwich—even though it takes twice the time—because she is very clear that it is what she wants to do and because it's good for her sense of her own capabilities, not to mention her fine motor skills. My seven-year-old puts on elaborate puppet-plays and at times I feel the urge to get to the dishes, but refraining allows me to appreciate her inventiveness and resourcefulness.

Deep Listening Within

When we move to fixing and rescuing we are also interrupting our children's ability to listen to their own wisdom, intuition, and natural ability to heal. We all have the capability to be insightful and self-aware and to self-heal. I believe that children can hone this ability to listen deeply and stay with their fear, to discover solutions, and to cope in ways that even we could not imagine.

In the celebrated book *How to Listen So Kids Will Talk and How to Talk So Kids Will Listen,* authors Adele Faber and Elaine Mazlish discuss the success they found in giving upset children a pen and paper and saying, "Write or draw how you feel." Kids would immediately calm down and creatively draw or diagram their emotional experience in a vivid way. So often when we go to fix, we shush them; we should say instead: "Your feelings are so important, I can see how upset you are—can you draw it for me so I can try to understand?" Art is a powerful way for kids to express what is inside of them, and more importantly, it gives kids an opportunity to listen inward and tap into their own abilities to process emotions.

Children's ability to listen deeply to their own selves sets them up for a lifetime of self-discovery and getting to know who they are. When children are distracted or redirected by parents every time they are upset, this too correlates to feelings of helplessness and depression.

Jack's Feelings

How do Jack's parents respond compassionately to his anxiety and refusal to go to school, while also encouraging him to do some deep listening to see if he has a solution to his own problem? Of course, as with most things, there isn't a quick fix, but the combination of compassion and deep listening can set this family on a healthier course.

Though Jack's parents are not stuck in bed with indecision, they have plenty of stress and anxiety of their own. They can feel and acknowledge their own human suffering and existence pain and validate that his pain is not only not silly, but rather quite important information. They can relate and perhaps share what they feel now or what they felt at times in their life when they too were stuck. They can ask if Jack knows what he is feeling. They can normalize and validate.

Here are some examples of compassionate communication:

- ▶ "It's okay to be worried. I worry a lot. Maybe you don't think I do, but I avoid a lot of things, just like you're avoiding getting dressed. I think avoidance is a fairly normal response. You know, I've even avoided whole sides of my family because I feel uncomfortable around them."
- ▶ "I sense that you do not like to feel worried or anxious and are trying to fight it. But worry is just an emotion like happiness is an emotion."
- ▶ "There is nothing wrong with you or your feelings. However, the behaviors you are choosing are not appropriate, because you're harming yourself by skipping school."
- ▶ "Anxiety is there all the time whether you stay in bed or not. I think you need to learn to navigate and cope with your anxiety and pain."

Deep listening may enable Jack to examine more closely what he is feeling. Here are some examples of ways to encourage it:

▶ "If you listen deeply, do you know what you are feeling?"

▶ "How would you like to address your anxiety? Do you want to stay in bed or try something else?"

▶ "If your anxiety could talk, what would it say? Can you draw it?"

▶ "What do you think is the best way to solve this?"

▶ "What do your instincts say—your inner voice?"

▶ "I am not going to keep coming in here to try to get you to go to school; I'm going to ask you to do some deep listening and come up with a solution yourself. However, if you still choose to not go to school, there will be consequences, such as no computer, and you may also have additional consequences from the school."

Compassion, reflective listening, refraining, validation, normalizing with boundaries, and consequences are all part of the moccasin-building process. Jack is more likely to process his emotions fluidly and less likely to get stuck in a behavior pattern with these parenting responses.

Using Thich Nhat Hanh's advice, how can we be alive, fresh, and present for our children—whether we know or understand their problem or not? Something like adoption pain, sexual identity, or even autism may take years to flush out or understand. There is a lot of unknown. Yet in the meantime we can practice being present, open, accepting, and compassionate to whatever our children are facing. We can be safe objects for our children.

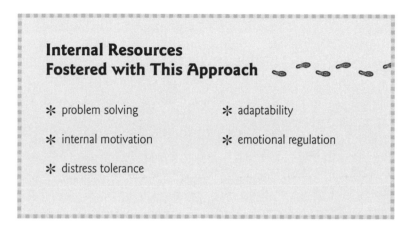

Internal Resources Fostered with This Approach

* problem solving
* internal motivation
* distress tolerance

* adaptability
* emotional regulation

CHAPTER 12

Skill: Removing the Leather
Brave Parenting

....

Vulnerability is the birthplace of innovation, creativity, and change.
—Brené Brown

....

When I was twenty, I lived in Africa for six months. I'd always known that was where I wanted to go, and my experiences there enriched me in many ways. The most treasured experience I took from living in Africa was also the most unexpected; I felt alive every day. I remember waking up and opening to life.

Every day was unpredictable. I didn't know what foods I would eat in any one day. I didn't know if the bus would run on time. I didn't know who I would meet. I didn't know if I would be able to get money from the bank; sometimes there were bureaucratic issues. I didn't know if I would be able to make a phone call; sometimes there were long lines. I didn't know if I could meet with an NGO, because I couldn't determine their office hours or phone numbers. I didn't know if I would get scammed (which happened), or if I would be invited into someone's home for tea (which frequently happened). I just took in every day—I didn't feel frustrated if something went wrong or if I couldn't accomplish something. I saw it all as part of my African experience.

Because there were so many unknowns, life felt exciting; it was an adventure. In fact, I felt my mental state was healthier, more flexible, and more open in Africa, though there was much to fear. I climbed Mt. Kilimanjaro, with only a hired guide; I hitched rides; I took a cargo ferry to Zanzibar and survived, though many people were seasick; I got an infection in my leg; I was asked to be married (a few times); I got jiggers (don't ask); I walked through Kibera, the second-largest urban slum in Africa. I was surrounded by threats, yet I didn't feel anxious. I felt more in touch with the pulse of human life and the natural world.

Here in the US, we expect everything to run like clockwork—as though we can completely control our environment. We get frustrated at any setback. Though life is more convenient and predictable in the United States, the predictability is actually quite dull. And despite this dullness we don't like any variations; we want to see everything that is coming. And we are still on guard, keeping alert for any hazard. This comes at a cost. What would happen if we opened up and embraced the unknown, shed our armor and lived each day to the fullest?

According to Buddhism, life is always in flux—even in developed countries. Impermanence underlies everything. Setbacks, disappointments, surprises, shifts are always happening. It's up to me to take my lessons from Africa and open up similarly to my life wherever I am. What if I took the mindset of my "African experience" and employed it all the time as the mindset for my "human experience?" Though I admit I'm not very good at this, when I do shift into this way of thinking, I feel more at ease and am in touch with a healthier mental state.

How can we teach kids to open up to the unknowns in life rather than to shut down and be anxious? How do we teach kids that staying present, right on the edge of the unknown, is where we feel most alive? How do we teach kids to stay with discomfort when it arises?

Brave Parenting

Surprisingly, in all my years as a guide and therapist, I never came across the word *brave* in the context of handling emotions until I began to study Buddhism. Therapy uses words like *cope, self-soothe, manage,* and *tolerate,* but these all have a slightly negative connotation; they're related to struggling with something hard. *Brave,* however, is a positive and powerful word. Especially considering the prevalence of the word *anxiety* and the explosion of anxiety disorders, why is there little talk about its opposite, bravery?

Tibetan Buddhist teacher Sakyong Mipham frequently teaches on bravery. He writes in "Confined by Cowardice" that bravery "is the act of wholeheartedly having the courage, relaxation, and insight simply to be. We arrive at this ability to be by cultivating a steady and forthright attitude toward the present moment." "Simply to be" means refraining from reacting to the present moment—refraining from closing down or spiraling out—and instead staying with the full spectrum of feelings, good and bad. What's interesting about his definition is that most of our anxiety is about the present moment—the uncertainty of what is coming next. He writes that we need a "steady and forthright attitude about the present moment." Rather than having another drink, reaching for caffeine, getting into bed, grabbing junk food, gossiping to a friend, finding distractions on the computer, or engaging in excessive planning, we should be brave and stay with the shaky feelings in the present moment.

In Africa this ability *to be* came more readily to me because I never knew what was coming next, yet in our comfortable lives in developed countries we construct in our minds what *should* be happening. We plan out our days in our heads and are upset at any variations. Yet being brave is not about control or eliminating fear—it is about accepting fear and getting to know it.

Bravery is like an old oak tree that sustains and grows storm after storm, season after season. How often do we simply ask our kids to be brave, to dig in their roots and sustain their storms? To feel the wind, hail, rain, snow, knowing that it will pass?

Children come into the world equipped with innate ways of processing feelings and enduring discomfort, and they all have the capacity to be brave. Instead of attempting to remove trouble, parents can allow their kids to struggle. When parents even join in by validating their child's highs and lows, parents are trusting their child's natural self-regulatory system—just like we trust the tree and its strong roots to sustain it. When children feel heard and validated by others, they feel supported, and most are ready to move on and solve their own problem.

Yet the parental responses for soothing, fixing, shushing, and placating seem to be hard-wired into all of us parents. I often find these programmed responses coming out of my mouth, despite my intentions to simply ask my children to be brave. However, when I do respond in an intentional way, I am shocked when my child comes up with some new, fresh perspective.

My older daughter once was in a local performance of *The Nutcracker*, and although she was nervous to be on a big stage, she really wanted to do it. At rehearsals she described strange feelings in her stomach—which we identified as nerves or "butterflies." She began to say more openly, "I am afraid." Trying to mirror and validate, I would say to her, "It is scary"; yet I also still snuck in the fix: "You'll do great." Yet when I tried to puff up her hope balloon in this way, it often seemed deflated.

The next time she brought up her worries again—which included falling, freezing on stage, forgetting what to do, or banging into someone with her headpiece—I took a risk by letting her be in charge of the problem and said, "It does sound scary. What do you think you'll do?" She hesitated and then said assuredly, "Well, I guess I'm just going to have to be brave." As I glanced over to her, wondering if I'd heard her correctly, there was a big smile on her face. She had solved her own problem.

Being brave has entered my parenting vocabulary. I talk about it all the time now—how do we be brave? One of my daughters was once told a scary story at her summer camp. Of course, when it came time to turn out the light that night, the scary images of the story seeped right into her consciousness and she became very worried about a green hand that was coming to get her. We talked about a few things; first, that it's totally okay to feel scared. That's what scary stories are for! And that she should just let herself feel scared, let the river of her emotions flow. Secondly, we discussed how she could transform the hand. Can the hand be something else—something that she loves and even wants to think about? After this short talk, she fell asleep. The next morning we talked about how brave she was—and that we can go to bed even if we feel scared.

Social rejection seems to just come with the territory of growing up. I have witnessed both of my girls being rejected right in front of me; interestingly, the two events were similar. In the first, my elder daughter spread her arms to hug a friend, who swiftly cold-shouldered her and turned away toward two other friends. My heart skipped a beat. Another time, my younger daughter saw two of her friends holding hands, and she went to grab one of their hands to join in on the fun; the girl shot her hand up in the air so my daughter could not hold it. These were hard to witness, but such occurrences are reality, and they happen daily for our kids.

These scenarios also created opportunities to talk about being brave and not letting another's behavior affect how we view ourselves. It is courageous to go out and make new friends and sit at a new lunch table. We can teach our children to keep opening their hearts, even when other kids close off to them.

Circus Smirkus

One summer, I experienced firsthand many brave children performing in a Vermont-based traveling circus called Circus Smirkus. These children, aged seven to eighteen, had completed sixty-four shows in seven weeks time and were frequently traveling away from their parents. But it took me a while to view it positively; at first I found myself judging Circus Smirkus: "Wow, I can't believe these kids are working all summer—at this grueling circus pace. I can't believe their parents let them do this. This is so dangerous!" There I was, hovering over my kids, making sure they stayed close to me, had enough snack and water, and were comfortable in their seats, all the while watching kids slightly older than my kids standing on adults' shoulders, doing flips, and performing, with their parents nowhere in sight.

But as I let the show sink in, I found myself stunned at their sheer talent, their joy, and particularly their bravery. It became clear to me that these children were on top of the world; rather than moving away from fear they lived in their fear by taking emotional and physical risks in front of an audience—and did so with, of course, big smiles on their face. It felt nothing short of miraculous. These children were living in their own bright lights.

Upon reading more about Circus Smirkus, my judgment subsided as I learned more about their mission and their focus on safety. Their philosophy is that you should compete with yourself and cooperate with others. It sounded so refreshing and down to earth, and clearly these kids were more than happy—they were having a blast.

When I left the show with my children, I felt the urge to let out their leash; let them stumble, fall, and get up on their own; let them take risks and live in their light; let them fail and succeed. After all, they are their own beings in the world. Life is short and no fun without getting a little messy. I felt braver after watching these kids, and I know my kids felt ready to take on the world.

Removing the Leather

Although children have their own temperaments and genetic makeup, they constantly read our cues about what's safe and what they should worry about. When we approach the world with fear and armor, our children will of course be affected by this; likewise, when we face fear openheartedly, our children will notice this as well. Fear will always exist. There is no such thing as being completely fearless. We all have fear about something. The issue is what we do with the fear—run away, armor up, numb out, find an escape, or go toward it.

How can we remove the leather around our children's feet? How can we let out the leash? How can we let our kids be in charge of their own lives, knowing they will make healthy and unhealthy choices and learn and grow in the process. How can we face our fears more openheartedly? These are some of tenets of brave parenting:

- ▶ *Accepting our children's approval and disapproval equally*, their happiness and their pain.
- ▶ *Allowing ourselves and our children to fail.* When we let ourselves fail, when we even make room for the possibility for it to happen—we are acknowledging fear and letting it be, instead of searching for control and security. Failure is a part of every person's life, and it does not mean we are good or bad. In Buddhism the word *failure* does not make sense because there is no ending or beginning; everything leads to something else. In the natural world there are sunny days and stormy days—they are not good or bad, they are both just textures of life.
- ▶ *Letting children feel with their hearts.* Our ability to feel and to love is what makes life worth living. You can have everything in the world and still have nothing if you have a closed heart. We can't shield our children from getting hurt—what we can do is allow them to feel and allow them to process feeling naturally. We can keep opening our hearts.

▶ *Encouraging risk-taking.* Kids will be more likely to take risks when they know mistakes and failure are okay and accepted. Risks allow us to actualize our potential and gifts—and develop who we are. When we take risks we feel more alive, just as I felt in Africa and as I observed at Circus Smirkus. Risk-taking is inherently different than recklessness. Recklessness is associated with running from or escaping pain, such as binge drinking and blacking out. Risk-taking is about going toward the pain, rather than away.

Becoming a Braver Parent:
Steps to Try at Home

1) Accept your child fully. Your child then will more easily accept him- or herself and become more dynamic and fluid in life, rather than rigid and stuck.

2) The next time your child complains, gives up, has a tantrum—let your child do it. Step out of the way. Let him have his own experience. Let her have her feeling. Free yourself from the feeling that it is your responsibility to fix.

3) Validate your child's feelings even if he or she is mad or angry with you.

4) Accept your child's most annoying habit and relate it to some personal struggle you have had in your life; this will help you talk about it more compassionately.

5) Do not tiptoe around your children's feelings; allow them to be upset.

6) Set limits on inappropriate behaviors and connect them to conse- quences. We'd rather our children experience small consequences in the home, than the unyielding consequences of the real world.

7) Allow your child to take a risk, knowing she may fail—life is about falling down and getting up.

8) Adopt a "no big deal" attitude.

9) Accept failure—even be grateful for it.

10) Ask your child to solve his or her own problem.

11) Ask your child to listen to his intuition, or inner wisdom, for an answer.

12) Always send two messages at once: accept all their feelings *and* set limits on their behaviors. For example, "I hear how angry you are. You're allowed to feel really mad at me, but you're not allowed to show disrespect."

13) Stop fixing.

14) Refrain, refrain, refrain.

15) Be gentle with yourself if you struggle with 1–14.

CONCLUSION
Contact with Nature

....

Nature has the power to transform and awaken us.
—**Mark Coleman,** *Awake in the Wild*

....

Halfway through a weekend meditation retreat with esteemed clinical psychologist and Buddhist teacher Tara Brach, Mother Nature made a grand entrance and turned everything upside down. A nor'easter hit before Halloween, settling a few feet of heavy wet snow on top of vibrant foliage and green lawns. Although Tara had been giving Dharma talks on being present, noticing others, looking into other's eyes, being vulnerable, and opening to the unknown, it did not seem like we fully embodied these concepts until we lost power, lit candles, entered the present moment, and genuinely felt a connection to others through the shared experience of being snowed in. Prior to the storm, I was shocked to see how many people clutched their handheld devices—despite it being a retreat atmosphere with strict rules regarding the use of screens. Yet after the storm, people were turning toward each other, putting down their devices, opening up to their coparticipants, and sharing shovels in the parking lot and flashlights in the bathrooms.

Mother Nature reminds us that we are all in the same boat, even though most of the time we forget this. When we feel a shared connection to others, we soften, we look beyond differences, and we *want* to get along. More importantly, when I stepped outside into the elements to see the glistening sunshine and the white wonderland, I was touched by something more powerful than the storm—the ever-present and enduring beauty of the natural world.

The nature-based metaphors and stories in this book can be reliable tenets for parenting any child today, whether in cities, suburbs, farms, or rural areas. Yet I would be remiss if I altogether skipped the importance of being in nature itself—and not just playing sports outside, going to a playground, the occasional ski trip, visiting zoos, or watching the nature channel. Children today need to have contact with the earth: to feel a sense of connection, to push up against natural limits, to explore their senses, to process their feelings, to be with the hum of the natural world instead of the electronic world.

We are creatures of nature, and we need to feel part of the natural world; research validates that this is actually critical for young people's mental health. Writer Richard Louv, who coined the term *nature-deficit disorder*, quotes a 2003 Cornell study in his book *Last Child in the Woods* that found that stressful events are less disturbing to children who live in high-nature conditions. Nancy Wells and Gary Evans, authors of the study, found that children with more nature in their lives exhibited less anxiety and depression and demonstrated more self-worth. Louv cites in his book studies that "confirm that one of the main benefits of spending time in nature is stress reduction."

The natural world has a way of slowing us down and taking our attention outside of ourselves. Mental health or emotional disturbances correlate to a degree of self-absorption. People who are depressed, anxious, or angry are turned inward, spinning storylines in their head or weighed down by overwhelming thoughts and feelings. The natural world can quickly disrupt this and snap people out of their heads and into the present moment. It might be the shrieking call of a crow, a brisk wind pressing against your face, a bright red tulip pushing up from thawing soil, a warm spring rain, or the scent of fresh snow on pine boughs. These sounds, smells, sights, and feelings grab our attention, even if temporarily. The natural world is a full-body experience and engages all of our senses, if we allow it. It is almost as if Mother Nature is grabbing us, shaking us, and saying, "Look outside yourself, you're part of a much larger web of life."

Many kids that are struggling are closed off, with eyes down, and are shut off from relationships. Frequently when kids feel upset, it's hard for them to engage with other people; adults, for instance, frequently want an explanation or to offer a solution. Nature does not expect anything or ask for anything back. As Thich Nhat Hanh explained, trees are present, fresh, and alive. Staying connected to the natural world is an important relationship for kids to maintain—especially when they are struggling in their human relationships. Animals also serve this purpose. A walk in the woods or a walk with a dog can be deeply healing and dramatically alter one's seemingly fixed perspective in the course of twenty minutes.

When we look up and out into the world and notice the rhythms of nature, we see the current of life that continues nonstop all around us. For a moment we can step outside ourselves; this is a relief. A teen in an indoor environment may simply reinforce her negative thoughts, because there is so much she can project. For example she may look in her closet and think, "I hate my clothes." She may look at her messy desk and feel overwhelmed with homework assignments. She may walk into school and think, "I don't fit in." She may wander through her house and feel a tension about what she "should" be doing. Indoor environments can reinforce thinking patterns—but stepping outside can open us up. When a teen looks up at the sky there may be no thought, projection, or reminder of who she is or what she needs to do. She may notice something outside herself: beautiful streaking clouds, dusk settling in, or a moon rising. The natural world is like a sponge that can soak up our stress and wring us out, so we come back indoors clearer and lighter and more focused.

When kids are cut off from all relationships, including a relationship with nature and animals, this is where depression and anxiety can really set in—because relationships with technology, computers, videos, and cell phones only reinforce anxiety and depression. In fact, I believe hand-held devices have come to represent the problems with our own brains. Thinking is of course an important human capacity: planning, analyzing, solving, and so on. Yet many of us think all day and all night long in mindless and unproductive ways that cause suffering and take us out of the present moment. Handheld computers have amazing capacities to access information and allow us to communicate with each other, yet they are also frequently misused, engaging us mindlessly, providing ceaseless distractions from life. We misuse both our own thinking brains as well as our created technology. This is largely because we have stepped so sharply away from nature.

Nature-Mature

It's not a surprise to me that the spelling of these two words, *nature* and *mature*, are so closely aligned. If I had to give one line of parenting advice, I think that it would be *if we want kids to mature, put them in nature*. Wilderness guide and psychologist Bill Plotkin writes in *Nature and the Human Soul* that nature "has always provided and still provides the best template for human maturation." To mature, he says, we need equal parts nature and culture—a balance that indigenous peoples and our ancestors who lived closer to the land achieved. I would argue that in Western childrearing today, nature plays less than 10 percent of a role in influencing children. Culture dominates children's lives, whether it is the culture of the family, school, community, or, most influential, mainstream culture. To become mature human beings, we have to increase our exposure to and relationship with the natural world.

The inherent limits of the natural world foster maturity in young people—kids have to be adaptable and have humility in outdoor settings. Whether we're working on a farm or ranch, backpacking, day hiking, sleeping in a tent, skiing, surfing, or simply going to a park, there are always elements outside of our control. Bugs, wet or frozen ground, rain, wind, hot or cold temperatures, rough waves—these rudiments of the natural world are always there. Yet these discomforts exist side-by-side with the joys of the natural world. So when we are in nature we have to soften, abide, acquiesce, and accept. This process is important for emotional maturation.

Nature also allows us to ponder the unknown. Our analytic minds search for answers and solutions to everything, but the natural world holds many mysteries, which perhaps allow us to stay with our own uncertainties.

In Alcoholic Anonymous, the central ingredient in people getting better and staying sober is a belief in a higher power. This "higher power" can be broadly defined, as many individuals in recovery are not Christian or even religious; they simply have to be willing to hand their lives over to a power that is greater than themselves. It doesn't matter if people look at the natural world in religious terms or not; the fact is when we look out the window we see a force that is greater than ourselves. Whether we look at the sun, the stars, the moon, or the earth itself, we see that we are quite small in comparison. When we discover that trees and turtles and many other living things live far beyond one hundred years, humans may seem transient in comparison. This recognition of a greater power in the natural world is not only humbling—it also helps restore sanity. When we see that there is a never-ending ebb and flow in life, we can more readily step away from trying to control our own life situations.

Back to Nature

A wilderness or other nature-based program is a good starting place for many struggling kids who need to reconnect to a full-sensory environment. These programs frequently entail rising with the sun and birds and finishing the day around the campfire—taking in the sounds and scents of a crackling fire, the rhythms of the flickering light, the quiet, dark evening and starry sky. Kids are outdoors all day soaking up healthy doses of vitamin D, natural exercise, hydration, healthy meals, and age-appropriate play. All of this has a stabilizing effect on our well-being. Living closer to the earth restores our own natural rhythms: breathing, sleeping, eating, exercising, and hydrating. Kids are more likely to stay with themselves, in their bodies and in their feelings.

Being in the natural world increases children's sensorial awareness. In natural environments kids can smell the earth, hear life around them, and capture a diversity of sights—all of which engages their full attention. Kids are responding to natural sounds, which are soothing, not the rings of cell phones or the beeps of texts. Self-judgments can fall to the wayside; there's a softening of external armor when kids are engaged in the present moment. When kids feel that they are part of something larger, they feel less isolated in their own self, their own pain. Kids are part of the living world. Moreover, self-consciousness subsides as kids get dirty and smelly, living close to Mother Earth.

Relationships with animals also serve the purpose of making contact with nature, as animals follow their own rhythms and are frequently great teachers themselves.

Mia

Mia is a therapy horse at a therapeutic ranch school in Wyoming. Mia herself is sassy, strong-willed, and at times stubborn—and so she is always paired up with the perfect self-absorbed, entitled, defiant, and closed-off child. When troubled Zach started at the ranch, it was clear that his primary coping skill was to shut down and give up when he was overwhelmed. He seemed to care little for others, specifically his parents, and he largely saw himself as a victim. He was good at blaming. The guides instantly knew Mia would be his horse.

Zach's responsibility was to be Mia's caretaker, which meant he had to feed her, groom her, and clean out her stall every day. Zach had no previous experience with horses; he was a city boy and was much more comfortable with his Xbox. When Zach showed up at the corral, Mia did not budge. Zach was closed off, his eyes were down, and he had an air of being bothered by this chore of feeding Mia. Well, Mia was going to have none of this. Most of the horses walk over and greet the teens who are their caretakers, but Mia walked away. Zach would have to go into the corral to be near her, sometimes in freezing rain or snow; to get anywhere with Mia he would have to rise up out of himself to engage. He had to drop the storylines in his head about how his suffering is someone else's fault and enter into the present moment. He had to surrender to her, because Mia would not respond to a self-absorbed teen.

Despite Mia's hardheadedness, Zach never skimped on his caretaking duties. He still tried to cut corners in many areas of the program, but he worried Mia would not eat unless he was there doing his chore. Deep down, he cared for her. And Mia also cared for him. When Zach was doing better, when he showed humility and was engaged and present, Mia would greet him. They had a nonverbal intimacy that was soothing to him. Yet when Zach was going through difficult periods with his parents and resumed his tendency to shutdown, Mia would lie down on the dirt, which is a significant gesture for a horse. She mirrored him. She held up her end of the relationship. She never worked harder than him, yet she accepted him unequivocally. Mia held him accountable.

When we work with animals or in the natural elements that are out of our control, we have to practice deep listening, attunement, and gratitude. Relationships with animals and nature are a gift. They take us out of our suffering and into the present moment. They connect us to life.

The Natural World and Making Moccasins

Impermanence is at the same time the most basic, enduring truth and the most challenging concept to grasp in our daily awareness. We constantly focus on security and certainty in order to feel safe, yet everything comes to an end and movement is constant. In our man-made world we try to "control" as much as possible—whether we program the thermostats of our homes, eat the same foods in winter as in summer, or escape to fabricated digital worlds. Through these actions, we lose touch with impermanence in everyday life. Once in a while we may experience more significant reminders such as a birth, a death, an illness, a marriage, or a job loss—but in the natural world, the reminders of impermanence are constant.

Whether leaves, snow, or rain are falling, change is constant. Author Mark Coleman writes in *Awake in the Wild* that "winds remind us again and again that there is ultimately nothing in this world that is permanent, that everything is in a state of flux. To live in harmony with this reality means cultivating an inner resilience and the ability to let go when circumstances inevitably change." Having direct daily experience with impermanence allows us to be more flexible and adaptable, which is part of the moccasin process.

Richard Louv cites that spending time in natural environments builds up natural confidence that kids may not get from other settings. He calls it "instinctual confidence." As there are real threats in outdoor settings, kids have to be more accountable and aware of immediate consequences: falling while crossing a creek, playing in poison ivy, getting lost, sunburn, and so on. This awareness develops children's senses and their ability to focus their attention. Focused attention and instinctual awareness are integral to the development of internal resources. Remember, we cannot control where our kids step, but we want them to hone their abilities to make sound decisions and solve their own problems; this happens naturally in outdoor settings.

Because it's hard to blame nature for a rainstorm, kids more readily process their feelings in natural settings and respond accordingly. Emotions come and go more quickly; it seems impossible for a child to stay stuck in a particular state in nature. Emotions stay fluid like water.

In nature, kids must employ delayed gratification—hiking to reach a summit, collecting firewood to make dinner, or simply waiting in a creek for the fish to bite. Problem solving and internal motivation instinctively happen when a strong wind hits a sailor, rain moves in on a rock climber, or a backpacker starts to run out of food. Self-discipline, distress tolerance, goal setting: these skills come with the territory if a child is to succeed in his or her outdoor pursuits.

When we encounter obstacles in natural settings, it would not make sense to ask someone else to fix or change it. The obstacles need to be endured, navigated, and mastered; no one can climb your boulders for you. But regardless of the struggle—muddy sections of a hiking trail, icy parts on the ski slope, hot sand on the beach, deep snow in the winter, or rocks on a bike path—it's usually still worth it to be outside. In fact, conquering obstacles is even fun.

Nature also provides a template for parenting. How can we let our children's obstacles stay on their path? How do we ask kids to stay with discomforts until they are endured or navigated? We can model for our children by being in nature ourselves, as well as valuing it for our children. We can also bring the lessons of nature indoors. The natural world keeps us on our toes, keeps us open to the unknown, and keeps our senses alert and present. This is the best model for allowing ourselves and our children to mature—to realize there are no shortcuts. In nature and in life each of us is alone in every moment. As parents, it is our responsibility to teach and model for our children how to make moccasins that will allow them to navigate the full range of experience that life will deliver.

Acknowledgments

I am grateful to have found the Buddhist teachings during my time of anxiety and insomnia. The wisdom of Pema Chodron and Chogyam Trungpa in the Shambhala tradition have provided much relief to both my sleeping and waking life. They have also allowed me to understand anxiety or fear, as it is expressed in our Western culture, in a way that psychology or therapy has been unable to.

I am grateful to my husband, Bob, for his never-ending support of me and my writing, as well as for his editorial feedback along the way. I am grateful to my mother, Ellie, for thoroughly reading my manuscript and providing validation, insight, and encouragement. I want to thank my friend Nicole for reading sections of the book and giving her wise insight and edits, as well as our long talks about parenting. I want to thank all my friends who are mothers whom I have engaged in endless conversations about parenting for emotional health; I want you all to know that your thoughts, insights, and perspectives were with me as I wrote this book. I also want to thank my daughters for their support and boundless love.

I am grateful to my agent, Dede Cummings, for her exuberant response to my book and for helping my book find a home at Wisdom Publications. I want to thank Laura Cunningham for her wise edits that have made my writing more crisp and accessible. And for helping me fine-tune the title.

Lastly, I am grateful to all the parents I have worked with and to all of my readers!

Bibliography

Arbinger Institute. *The Anatomy of Peace: Resolving the Heart of Conflict.* San Francisco: Bernett-Koehler Publishers, 2008.

Barrows, Anita, and Joanna Macy, trans. *Rilke's Book of Hours: Love Poems to God.* New York: Riverhead Trade, 2005.

Bly, Robert. "The Long Bag We Drag Behind Us." In *Meeting the Shadow: The Hidden Power of the Dark Side of Human Nature*, edited by Connie Zweig and Jeremiah Abrams. New York: Tarcher/Putnam, 1991.

Brach, Tara. *Radical Acceptance: Embracing Your Life with the Heart of the Buddha.* New York: Bantam Books, 2003.

Chodron, Pema. *No Time to Lose: A Timely Guide to the Way of the Bodhisattva.* Boston: Shambhala Publications, 2005.

———. *When Things Fall Apart: Heart Advice for Difficult Times.* Boston: Shambhala Publications, 1997.

Coleman, Mark. *Awake in the Wild: Mindfulness in Nature as a Path of Self-Discovery.* Maui: Inner Ocean Publishing, 2006.

The Dalai Lama. *Advice on Dying: And Living a Better Life.* New York: Atria, 2002.

The Dalai Lama. *An Open Heart: Practicing Compassion in Everyday Life.* Edited by Nicholas Vreeland. New York: Little Brown and Company, 2001.

Epstein, Mark. *Going to Pieces Without Falling Apart: A Buddhist Perspective on Wholeness.* New York: Broadway, 1998.

Hofer, Barbara, and Abigail Sullivan Moore. *The iConnected Parent: Staying Close to Your Kids in College (and Beyond) While Letting Them Grow Up.* New York: Free Press, 2010.

Louv, Richard. *Last Child in the Woods: Saving Our Children from Nature-Deficit Disorder.* New York: Algonquin Books, 2008.

Magid, Barry. *Nothing Is Hidden: The Psychology of Zen Koans*. Boston: Wisdom Publications, 2013.

McKinnon, John. *An Unchanged Mind: The Problem of Immaturity in Adolescence*. New York: Lantern Books, 2008.

Mipham, Sakyong. "Confined by Cowardice." *Shambhala Sun*, March 2011.

Mogel, Wendy. *Blessings of a Skinned Knee: Using Jewish Teachings to Raise Self-Reliant Children*. New York: Scribner, 2008.

Morinaga, Soko. *Novice to Master: An Ongoing Lesson in the Extent of My Own Stupidity*. Boston: Wisdom Publications, 2004.

Nelson, Margaret. *Parenting Out of Control: Anxious Parents in Uncertain Times*. New York University Press, 2010.

Piaget, Jean. *The Psychology of the Child*. New York: Basic Books, 1972.

Plotkin, Bill. *Nature and the Human Soul: Cultivating Wholeness and Community in a Fragmented World*. Novato, CA: New World Library, 2008.

Shantideva. *The Way of the Bodhisattva*. Boston: Shambhala Publications, 1997.

Siegal, Daniel, and Mary Hartzell. *Parenting From the Inside Out: How a Deeper Self-Understanding can Help You Raise Children Who Thrive*. New York: Tarcher/Penguin, 2003.

Thich Nhat Hanh. "Be Beautiful, Be Yourself." *Shambhala Sun*, January 2012.

Trungpa, Chogyam. *Smile at Fear: Awakening the True Heart of Bravery*. Boston: Shambhala Publications, 2010.

Weil, Andrew. *Spontaneous Happiness*. New York: Little Brown, 2011.

Weissbourd, Richard. *The Parents We Mean to Be: How Well-Intentioned Adults Undermine Children's Moral and Emotional Development*. Boston: Mariner Books, 2009.

Yalom, Irvin. *Love's Executioner: Other Tales of Psychotherapy*. New York: Perennial Classics, 1989.

Index

Page numbers followed by "q" indicate quotations.

About the Author

 Krissy Pozatek, LICSW, is an author, speaker, licensed therapist, and parent coach. She speaks and facilitates transformational parent workshops all over the country. Krissy was educated at Middlebury College, Smith College, and New Mexico Highlands University and is the author of *The Parallel Process: Growing Alongside Your Adolescent or Young Adult in Treatment*. She lives in Vermont with her husband and two daughters. You can learn more about her work at www.parallel-process.com.

About Wisdom Publications

Wisdom Publications is the leading publisher of contemporary and classic Buddhist books and practical works on mindfulness. Publishing books from all major Buddhist traditions, Wisdom is a nonprofit charitable organization dedicated to cultivating Buddhist voices the world over, advancing critical scholarship, and preserving and sharing Buddhist literary culture.

To learn more about us or to explore our other books, please visit our website at www.wisdompubs.org. You can subscribe to our eNewsletter or request our print catalog online, or by writing to:

Wisdom Publications
199 Elm Street
Somerville, Massachusetts 02144 USA

You can also contact us at 617-776-7416, or info@wisdompubs.org.

Wisdom is a 501(c)(3) organization, and donations in support of our mission are tax deductible.

Wisdom Publications is affiliated with the Foundation for the Preservation of the Mahayana Tradition (FPMT).